SAS

GULF WARRIORS

SAS
GULF WARRIORS

STEVE CRAWFORD

SIMON & SCHUSTER
A VIACOM COMPANY

First published in Great Britain by Simon & Schuster Ltd, 1995
A Viacom Company
Copyright © Brown Packaging 1995

The right of Brown Packaging Ltd to be identified as authors
of this work has been asserted by them in accordance with the Copyright,
Designs and Patents Act, 1988.

Simon & Schuster Ltd
West Garden Place
Kendal Street
London W2 2AQ

Simon & Schuster of Australia Pty Ltd
Sydney

A CIP catalogue record for this book is available from the British Library

ISBN 0-671-51216-1

Editorial and design:
Brown Packaging Limited
255-257 Liverpool Road, London, N1 1LX

Printed and bound in Great Britain by
Butler and Tanner Limited
Selwood Printing Works
Caxton Road, Frome,
Somerset, BA11 1NF

Extracts taken from 'Bravo Two Zero' by Andy McNab (Bantam Press,
London 1993) and from 'The One That Got Away' by Chris Ryan
(Century, London 1995)

This book is dedicated to the memory of my grandfather,
who during his service life endured dangers and hardships
greater than those described in this book.

CONTENTS

CHAPTER 1

Born in the Desert

The Special Air Service (SAS) has a long association with the desert. Indeed, it was born in the desert in World War II, the brainchild of a young Scots Guards officer named David Stirling. When it comes to desert warfare, therefore, the SAS has a pedigree matched by very few other special forces units. It was thus logical that Britain's élite would be despatched to Arabia when Iraq seized Kuwait.

This book is about the campaign conducted by the men of the British Special Air Service (SAS) during the 1991 Gulf War, waged by those multinational forces acting on behalf of the resolutions passed at the United Nations (UN) regarding the forceful removal of Iraqi troops from Iraqi-occupied Kuwait. For the SAS, the war resulted in the largest concentration of its soldiers on the ground since World War II, and in the end the whole British special forces group totalled 700 men.

On 2 August 1990, over 100,000 Iraqi troops, accompanied by 1000 tanks and led by six divisions of the elite Republican Guard, invaded the oil-rich state of Kuwait. Why did Iraq desire Kuwait? The answer lies in the fact that Iraq, in the aftermath of her recently concluded eight-year war with Iran, had an $80 billion debt accumulated as a consequence of having to fight that war. Saddam Hussein, the Iraqi dictator, believed with some justification that his country had prevented the spread of Shiite fundamentalism throughout the Middle East, and had directly saved the ruling royal families of Kuwait and Saudi Arabia. However, after the war's end Kuwait insisted that Iraq repay the $65 billion loan she owed. This did nothing to endear Kuwait or the Kuwaitis to the Baathist regime in Baghdad. Furthermore, Kuwait herself had massive financial reserves at home and abroad, and that wealth could obviously resolve Iraq's financial problems.

Opposite: An SAS soldier loads rounds into a Vickers machine gun magazine during the campaign in the North African desert in 1942.

Iraq also accused Kuwait of extracting oil from the Rumaila oil field, which lay in a disputed tract of territory on the two countries' common border. To add final insult to existing injury, Kuwait was engaged in the over-production of oil. This had the effect of depressing oil prices, which further aggravated Iraq's inability to service its debt. Saddam Hussein accused Kuwait and the United Arab Emirates of depriving Iraq of $14 billion of oil revenue. He openly threatened Kuwait, and he was pushed over the edge

Above: Iraqi tanks move through the deserted streets of Kuwait City during Saddam Hussein's invasion of Kuwait. Iraqi T-72s had brushed aside feeble resistance at the border, shooting up Kuwaiti infantry armed only with small arms.

when the Emir of Kuwait refused to meet him in face-to-face talks to resolve the predicament, preferring instead Arab League mediation.

It was not just about oil. Iraq and Kuwait, both formerly part of the Ottoman Empire, shared a common border that had never been properly defined. Turkish rule was replaced by a British mandate over the two at the end of World War I, but the border problem was never resolved. Indeed, an old Iraqi claim is that Kuwait is in fact an integral part of Iraq.

Saddam Hussein believed that a swift and, if necessary, violent invasion of Kuwait would give him de facto possession of the state and would in effect present the international community with a fait accompli. He believed that the UN in particular would bluster for a time, but that in the

Below: An amateur video showing Kuwaiti light armoured vehicles defending the Dasman Palace, the residence of the Emir of Kuwait, several hours after the Iraqi invasion. Such gallant resistance was useless against Iraqi forces.

SAS GULF WARRIORS

Above: Smoke rises behind the Kuwaiti Towers on 2 August 1990 – the date of the Iraqi invasion. As well as armoured and mechanised units, the Iraqis also made use of amphibious and heliborne troops to crush Kuwaiti resistance.

Although in retrospect Saddam's actions were entirely misjudged, at the time the Iraqi dictator had good reason to believe that he could get away with his plan. For example, the signals that the United States in particular sent to Baghdad in the months before the invasion were confusing to say the least. On 17 July, Saddam had threatened to use force to resolve his disputes with his neighbours. Two days later the US ambassador in Baghdad, April Glaspie, under orders from the Secretary of State James Baker, stated that 'disputes should be settled by peaceful means, not through intimidation.' It was a clear enough signal, perhaps, but five days later Glaspie delivered another message from Baker, which repeated the plea for a peaceful resolution of disputes, but which also informed Saddam that the USA had 'no opinion on the Arab-Arab conflicts, like your border disagreement with Kuwait.'

Such language was hardly the green light for Saddam to send his troops south, or rather that is how it was perceived in the USA and other Western democracies. Nevertheless, such things have rarely bothered the Iraqi leader. The former SAS commander and subsequent leader of all the British forces in the Gulf, Lieutenant-General Peter de la Billière, has written succinctly about Saddam: 'a brutal dictator who ruled through fear and treated human beings as expendable pawns in pursuit of his own ambition... If not clinically insane, he was at least irrational and therefore dangerously unpredictable.'

These words were to ring true at the beginning of August 1990, as Iraqi troops poured into Kuwait and began the systematic looting of the country. In the face of this aggression, the international community, with the USA in the van, rapidly organised a response. As strongly worded

end Kuwait would become the nineteenth province of Iraq, thereby increasing his prestige and fearsome reputation in the Gulf, and at the same time give Iraq access to Kuwait's oil fields.

resolutions demanding the immediate withdrawal of Iraqi forces from Kuwait poured forth from the United Nations (UN Security Council Resolution 678 of 29 November 1990, for example, authorised the removal of Iraqi forces from Kuwait by 'all necessary means'), a military force began to assemble in Saudi Arabia. In late August 1990, General Norman Schwarzkopf, commanding general of the US Central Command and

Above: Iraqi armour in Kuwait City after its fall to Saddam Hussein. The latter installed one of his cousins to rule the city. Ali Hassan al-Majid moved 7000 members of the Iraqi secret police into the city, and then began a reign of terror.

now United Nations theatre commander-in-chief, arrived in Riyadh and began planning the immediate defence of Saudi Arabia and the ultimate liberation of Kuwait.

SAS GULF WARRIORS

No one really knew if Saddam would attempt to occupy the vast oil fields of Saudi Arabia farther south (Hussein himself probably did not know, as his thoughts were rarely rational and many of his actions were pure whims). By early September 1990, however, the Americans had at least assembled a force large enough to make him think twice about any such escapade. By that time there were seven US Army brigades, three aircraft carrier battle groups, 14 fighter squadrons and 17,000 US Marines in the Gulf, and a squadron of Boeing B-52 Stratofortress strategic heavy bombers had arrived on the island of Diego Garcia in the Indian Ocean.

As the Iraqis began to entrench in Kuwait, thousands of troops from many nations arrived in Saudi Arabia under the United Nations banner. Soldiers from the United Kingdom, Italy, France, Canada, Australia, Belgium, the Netherlands, Spain, Denmark, Norway, South Korea, Greece, Portugal, Argentina, Bangladesh, Morocco, Egypt, Senegal, Pakistan, Oman, Niger and Saudi Arabia began to prepare for the offensive that would drive the Iraqis out of Kuwait. The British contingent, under the operational codename 'Granby', eventually numbered 45,000, though it was only 14,000 at the beginning of November 1990. The overall British commander in the Gulf, as noted above, was Lieutenant-General Peter de la Billière.

An SAS veteran of nearly 40 years, de la Billière was admirably qualified to lead the British contingent. Having had much experience of serving in the Middle East (he had a knowledge of the Arabic language, for example), he had worked as Commander of British Forces and Military Commissioner in the Falkland Islands in the 1980s, which had given him invaluable

Above: David Stirling, the man responsible for the creation of the Special Air Service. He laid down the principles on which the Regiment is still based, and gathered around him men who embodied those principles. He died in 1990.

experience of tri-service command. From the SAS's point of view, his service with the Regiment would prove beneficial in securing a role for SAS troops in the war, as well as allaying

Schwarzkopf's fears and distrust of special forces soldiers. Peter de la Billière's career read like an adventure novel. He was originally commissioned into the Durham Light Infantry, but joined the SAS as a captain in Malaya in 1955, and fought in the campaign against the insurgents there. Between December 1958 and January 1959, he served with the SAS in Oman, taking part in the famous Jebel Akhdar operation (when the SAS dislodged and defeated a group of rebels ensconced on a high mountain plateau in northern Oman; the operation was all the more remarkable because the position was reckoned to be impregnable). He then fought in the British debacle in Aden, eventually serving as a major commanding an SAS squadron. Then came the repulse of Indonesian territorial ambitions in Borneo, where he was awarded the Military Cross and Bar. Success followed success, as he subsequently rose to command 22 SAS Regiment itself and then become Director of Special Forces (DSF), a London-based position commanding both the SAS and the Special Boat Service (SBS), and all other agencies associated, or working in support of, special forces operations. While the title is still listed as DSF, the administrative title is now Director Advanced Forces. During the Falklands War in 1982, Brigadier de la Billière ensured that the SAS was included in the campaign, believing, rightly as it transpired, that the Regiment's talents would be needed in the South Atlantic. He would have this conviction again eight years later in Saudi Arabia, and once again he would be proved right. Above all, de la Billière was a no-nonsense gifted commander, in whose hands the British force was handled with skill and élan. And the SAS had a friend in high places.

That the SAS would be deployed to the Gulf in 1990 was perhaps inevitable, for it was one of the few special forces units in the world that had 50 years' experience of desert operations. And though Schwarzkopf may have been suspicious of special forces in general, a consequence of his experiences as a commander on the ground in Vietnam, it is unlikely that he would have refused the help of such a seasoned unit, laying aside de la Billière's urgings. His belief with regard to élite units were that they were unreliable, that they often promised more than they could deliver, and that at the end of the day considerable resources were tied up with extracting them from the messes into which they got themselves. The list of US special forces failures was long and salutory. Two examples are the abortive Delta Force attempt to rescue American hostages in Tehran in 1980, and the laughable operation conducted by the same unit during the American invasion of Grenada three years later: the heliborne Delta team was tasked with rescuing prisoners held in Richmond Hill prison on Grenada, but as a result of poor planning arrived in daylight rather than under cover of darkness, and spent the day pinned down under enemy fire and had itself to be rescued. However, when he looked at the pedigree of the SAS, Schwarzkopf found a different story.

The origins of the SAS lay in the North African desert in 1941

The origins of the SAS lay in the North African desert in 1941, and with a young Scots Guards officer named David Stirling. Stirling took part in a number of British commando operations against Axis targets on the North African coast. These were mostly large-scale affairs and rather ineffectual. As a result, Stirling began to formulate in his mind the most effective ways to strike at the enemy. He came up with the idea that a number of small-sized teams (200 men split into five-man squads) would be much more effective than one large-scale mission, which also had the disadvantage of tying up a number of Royal Navy ships. Far better to hit the enemy at many points, Stirling reasoned, so at least the chances of success would be increased.

Stirling's audacity paid off and he was promoted to captain and ordered to form his unit

These ideas remained in Stirling's head until, fortuitously for the future of the SAS though not so good for young Stirling himself, he was involved in a parachute accident that put him in hospital. While he was lying, in some agony, in his hospital bed, he put his thoughts down onto paper and decided to present them to his superiors. In this he had a problem: the levels of bureaucracy that he as a junior officer would have to penetrate would inevitably result in his ideas being stillborn (Stirling endearingly called these channels the 'fossilised shit'). He therefore decided to go directly to the Commander-in-Chief Middle East, General Sir Claude Auchinleck. Walking with the aid of his crutches he managed to bluff his way past the guards at the gates and got himself into the building that housed Auchinleck's office. Dodging guards and staff officers alike, he was finally cornered in the office of Auchinleck's deputy chief of the general staff, Major-General Neil Ritchie. Quickly introducing himself

before he was escorted from the compound, Stirling handed Ritchie his hastily scribbled notes and briefly informed the somewhat surprised senior officer of his ideas. Equally surprisingly, perhaps, Ritchie promised to read them and pass them on to Auchinleck.

Stirling's audacity (some would say impertinence) paid off: he was promoted to captain and ordered to form his new command. It was grandly called L Detachment, Special Air Service Brigade, and it was born in July 1941 (HQ Middle East dreamed up this name to deceive the Germans into believing that a new airborne brigade had been created – L Brigade had in fact 67 men at its birth). Thus was the SAS born, and its first base was at Kabrit, near the Suez Canal.

Very soon the SAS was staffed by individuals who possessed those personal qualities that have since become synonymous with the Regiment. The founding principles of the SAS were laid down by Stirling himself. These were the never-ending pursuit of excellence; the maintenance of the highest standards of self-discipline in every aspect of military life; the toleration of no sense of class as all ranks in the SAS were to be one family; and all ranks to possess a sense of humour and humility. Under the command of Stirling, and with training conducted under the watchful eye of Captain 'Jock' Lewes, the SAS began to take shape in the desert. Many of the early recruits quickly became legends in the Regiment. They subsequently became known as the 'Originals', men such as Johnny Cooper, the wild Irishman 'Paddy' Mayne, Reg Seekings and Bob Bennett. Training at Kabrit was for one purpose only: to prepare the recruits for the tasks of acting independently in small groups or as individuals behind the lines, and of being able to

live off the land and fend for themselves. Above all, this kind of work called for the highest levels of self-discipline, thus anyone unsuitable was immediately sent back to his original unit.

Although the SAS's first operation in November 1941 was a complete disaster, largely because the men were dropped by parachute miles from their drop zone and in appalling weather that made assembly on the ground impossible, the

Above: The SAS's campaign in Malaya during the 1950s saw the Regiment learn jungle warfare and counter-insurgency skills. In addition, the SAS's Selection and Continuation courses were established back in England.

nature of the war in North Africa during World War II was ideally suited to small-sized teams working behind the lines, a lesson reinforced 50 years later in Kuwait and Iraq. The campaign in

SAS GULF WARRIORS

Above: Back to the Middle East. The picture shows an SAS Browning 0.5in heavy machine gun used against rebels during the Jebel Akhdar operation in late 1958. SAS soldiers were flown directly from Malaya to dislodge the insurgents, and had to acclimatise very quickly to the terrain.

North Africa was dominated by supply lines, notably the roads located, for the most part, near the coast. The Axis and Allied armies were entirely dependent on depots, ports and airstrips to keep them supplied with fuel, supplies, war

material and reinforcements. By the end of 1941, Axis supply lines were very long as a result of Rommel's successes. This meant there were many lightly defended targets in the enemy's rear that were vulnerable. If they could be attacked it would damage the enemy's ability to wage war, as well as draw away front-line troops to guard them.

Immediately after the failed first mission, Stirling, undeterred, came to an agreement with the British Long Range Desert Group (LRDG), an intelligence-gathering and reconnaissance unit, whereby the LRDG would transport SAS soldiers to and from their targets in its vehicles. This was an inspired idea, and in December 1941 the truck-mounted SAS conducted its first raids against five enemy airfields behind the lines. The result was that nearly 100 Axis aircraft were destroyed on the ground. The SAS was in business! Subsequent raids hit enemy ports, supply dumps and more airfields, and dozens more aircraft were destroyed in their neatly parked rows on the ground. In 1942 the SAS acquired its own transport in the shape of American jeeps, which were liberally equipped with machine guns. By the end of the North

African campaign in May 1943, the SAS had achieved some spectacular successes, and numbered 600 men in two regiments. Though the war, and with it the SAS, then moved away from the desert, the Regiment would return to the Middle East 15 years later.

The ideas of David Stirling were refined and continued in Malaya

The SAS fought with distinction in northwest Europe and Italy in 1943-45, but in the immediate post-war future it looked as though it would become another illustrious wartime unit that would be disbanded. However, a campaign of terror and subversion waged by communist guerrillas in Malaya beginning in 1948 resulted in 22 SAS being reformed in 1952. After a shaky start with regard to discipline and tactics, the SAS proved itself to be adept at long-range operations in tropical jungle terrain. The ideas of David Stirling were refined and continued in Malaya by men such as Brigadier 'Mad' Mike Calvert, an SAS veteran of World War II, and Lieutenant-Colonel John Woodhouse. The former devised tactics for jungle operations, and introduced the 'hearts and minds' concept into the Regiment's operational skills. The 'hearts and minds' concept, in which SAS soldiers gain the trust of locals by learning their language, customs and sharing in their lifestyle, often living with locals for months at a time, is now an integral part of SAS counter-insurgency warfare methods.

John Woodhouse, now regarded as the father of the modern SAS, worked with the Regiment in Malaya and always insisted on the highest levels of physical and mental discipline and fitness.

He correctly recognised that the key to ensuring that the Regiment's soldiers were up to scratch was the selection and training process. He therefore returned to England in 1952 to organise SAS recruitment procedures.

The present SAS Selection and Continuation Training courses are basically the same as those devised by John Woodhouse back in the 1950s, and their endurance is testimony to his vision over 40 years ago.

Missions mainly consisted of establishing observation posts to keep an eye on the enemy

---

With the aid of the SAS the British authorities in Malaya won the counter-insurgency war, and forced the rebels to withdraw into neighbouring Thailand, never again to present a threat to the government in Kuala Lumpur. By 1958 the SAS contained seasoned jungle fighters, but their next task was to fight in the barren, rocky expanses of northern Oman, on behalf of the ruling sultan, the aged Said bin Taimur. As a result of her imperial adventures, the UK in the post-war world had ties to many Third World states. Oman was one such country. Treaties between the sultan and the British government had first been signed in the 18th century, and ties of mutual benefit had been, and indeed still are, continued and encouraged by both sides. When a rebellion broke out in his country and he was unable to suppress it with his own troops, the sultan called upon the British for help. The latter sent an infantry brigade, which pushed the rebels onto the plateau of the so-called Jebel Akhdar, the Green Mountain. There the rebels stayed, secure on their plateau surrounded by high peaks.

Conventional forces were ill-suited to take such a stronghold, so the British Government dispatched the SAS. In November 1958, 70 men of D Squadron arrived in Oman and took up position around the plateau and began probing rebel positions. A Squadron arrived at the beginning of the new year and the decision was taken to make a determined push against the rebels. The decisive offensive occurred in late January 1959, when an SAS attack stormed the plateau and forced the rebels to surrender. The Jebel Akhdar operation remains a classic example of how a small elite unit, if superbly fit and well led, can achieve results out of all proportion to its size. It was also an indication of how SAS soldiers could fight in any terrain at small notice: one week in the humid jungles of Malaya, the next in the searing heat of the Arabian desert.

The next return to the desert came in April 1964, when SAS soldiers were despatched to the crown colony of Aden. The previous year the Regiment had started its campaign in Borneo, which was to end far more happily than the one in Aden. Nevertheless, the war in the latter did have benefits for the Regiment of a long-term nature: it marked the beginning of the SAS's counter-terrorist capability. The actual campaign against Yemeni-backed insurgents in the Radfan of Aden was frustrating for the Regiment. The first operation in April 1964 ended in failure, and the head of one of the SAS junior commanders, Captain Robin Edwards, was displayed in the Yemeni town of Taiz. Subsequent missions were rather better planned and executed as A, B and D Squadrons were rotated through Aden. Missions mainly consisted of establishing observation posts in the hinterland to keep an eye on enemy movements. In the port of Aden itself, SAS sol-

diers conducted plainclothes counter-insurgency (COIN) work, infiltrating into the town in so-called 'Keeni Meeni' operations against Yemeni-trained assassins. It was dangerous and often frustrating work, and ultimately unsuccessful as the British had decided to pull out of the colony and leave it to its fate. This they did in November 1967. Nevertheless, the basis of the Regiment's counter-terrorist techniques had been laid, and

Above: Members of 16 Troop, D Squadron, 22 SAS, photographed on the Jebel Akhdar on 28 January 1959, the day after the operation that effectively defeated the rebels. The assault was one of the SAS's greatest achievements.

these skills would be refined and developed in later years back in England.

A much more successful campaign was waged by the Regiment between 1970 and 1976, when once again SAS soldiers were called upon to support the Omani regime. If the war in the north of Oman was fought in the mountains, this one was conducted in the sand and gravel of Dhofar, a province in the south of the country. It proved, if proof were in fact needed, that the SAS could wage and win a counter-insurgency war, not so much through the barrel of a gun but by the intelligent application of well thought-out and timely civil aid policies.

The SAS arrived none too soon, for the sultan's forces were on the verge of collapse

---

Aside from the mountains, much of Oman resembles Iraq and Kuwait, i.e. large expanses of inhospitable desert. As a result the indigenous population is poor, a problem made worse during the reign of Said bin Taimur by his autocratic rule. His repressive methods had resulted in the outbreak of rebellion in Dhofar in 1962 – a largely small-scale affair that posed little threat to his rule. The rebel group, the Dhofar Liberation Front, was basically conservative in outlook and had limited aims. However, it was gradually taken over by the more radical People's Front for the Liberation of the Occupied Arabian Gulf (PFLOAG), a communist group backed up by the recently formed People's Democratic Republic of Yemen, plus the USSR and China. This made the rebels, or *adoo* as they became known, a much more potent threat, and the sultan's forces proved woefully inept at waging a full-scale counter-insurgency war, or indeed a counter-insurgency war at all. The result was inevitable: by 1970 the rebels had control of the whole of the Jebel Dhofar and the government

was in full retreat. Once again the sultan called upon the British for aid, and once again the SAS was detailed to solve the crisis.

In fact, the SAS had been in Oman since 1969, when a troop had arrived to begin training the sultan's forces. The commander of 22 SAS at that time, Lieutenant-Colonel Johnny Watts, realised though that his men could do little unless Said bin Taimur was removed, for it was his presence and his policies that were pushing the inhabitants of Dhofar into the hands of the rebels (the sultan's repressive measures were harsh, and ranged from flogging and imprisonment for the slightest transgressions to the sealing of wells as a punishment for entire village communities). Clearly the sultan would have to go if Oman was to be prevented from becoming another Yemen, but it was beyond the remit of the SAS to instigate such a course. However, fate was on the side of the men who wore the Winged Dagger, for the sultan's more enlightened son, Qaboos, had the same thoughts and in a virtually bloodless palace coup in 1970 overthrew his father (the coup was not entirely bloodless for Sultan Said bin Taimur managed to shoot himself in the foot during all the excitement!).

Within hours of the coup an SAS team arrived in Dhofar, although it was officially known as a British Army Training Team (BATT) so that the British Government could deny that its troops were actively engaged in Oman. The soldiers arrived none too soon, for the sultan's forces were on the first of collapse. They were confined to a few coastal towns such as Salalah, Rakyut, Taqa and Mirbat, and the rebels controlled most of the hinterland. In Watts' mind there was only one way to reverse the situation: wage a 'hearts and minds' campaign to win back the Dhofaris.

He formulated a plan, called the 'Five Fronts' campaign, to achieve this.

The 'Five Fronts' plan called for the counter-insurgency war to be conducted on five fronts. First, an intelligence cell would be created to gather accurate information about the enemy, the Sultan's Armed Forces (SAF) and the locals. Second, an information team would disseminate accurate information to the indigenous population regarding SAS aims and the policies of Sultan Qaboos, as opposed to propaganda. Third,

and most importantly, the SAS would make medical expertise available to the locals (in this way it was hoped that the populace would grow to trust the SAS soldiers; it was also hoped that the Regiment could gather valuable intelligence through local gossip). Fourth, the SAS would

Below: Between 1964-67 the Regiment fought Yemeni- and Egyptian-backed rebels in the Radfan. SAS teams would establish observation posts at night, from where artillery and air strikes could be directed against the enemy.

SAS GULF WARRIORS

provide veterinary facilities for the indigenous population. Fifth, and finally, the SAS would endeavour to enlist Dhofaris to fight for the sultan. All these measures were sanctioned by Qaboos himself, who aided the SAS by granting a general amnesty in the late summer of 1970. Even so, it was a tall order to fulfil, and in 1970 the odds were stacked against success.

So the first SAS-trained irregular unit, called a **firqat**, was formed

More SAS troops were sent to Oman in September 1970 to enable more BATTs to be established, and fate again smiled upon the SAS in the shape of a rebel leader, Salim Mubarak, who, together with his followers, had fought their way off the Jebel Dhofar and surrendered to the authorities (the PFLOAG were alienating many of its Dhofari recruits by its anti-Muslim policies). As a result, the SAS had its first potential Dhofari recruits. Urgent talks with the sultan acquired royal assent, and so the first SAS-trained irregular unit, called a *firqat*, was formed. It was called the *Firqat Salahadin*, after the great Muslim leader, and was the first of several such units.

Meanwhile, the civil aid programme proceeded apace. New wells were drilled and medical aid was given to people and their animals alike. All the time SAS soldiers were quick to stress that they were only laying the foundation for work that would be continued by the Omanis them-

Right: SAS men unload supplies from an RAF Beverley transport aircraft during the war in Oman. The Regiment's 'hearts and minds' campaign was the key to success in the conflict, establishing bonds of trust with the locals.

selves once the SAS had left their country. In this way the Dhofaris slowly became convinced that the government and the sultan genuinely wished to help them.

A major turning point in the war occurred on 19 July 1972 at the town of Mirbat

On the military front, the SAS, SAF and *firqats* began to launch missions against the *adoo*. These missions were on a small scale at first, but more ambitious operations were undertaken as success bolstered the morale of regular and irregular units alike. The war was taken to the guerrillas, and, despite some minor setbacks, by the end of 1971 the government had made substantial gains: the coastal plain and towns were under Omani control, there was a government presence on the jebel and there were 700 Dhofaris fighting in *firqats*. However, a major turning point in the war occurred on 19 July 1972 at the town of Mirbat, when the SAS achieved a military victory that has since become a legend.

SAS soldiers may be able to converse in many tongues, to administer medical treatment and operate sophisticated communications equipment, but at the bottom of it all they are still highly trained and motivated soldiers who can handle their weapons with great dexterity. They are trained to win firefights and battles using a combination of maximum firepower allied to ammunition conservation. On that July day over 250 *adoo* attacked Mirbat and its defenders: nine SAS men together with a few armed tribesmen and armed police. At the end of the battle, though, for the loss of two SAS men dead, there were dozens of *adoo* dead on the battlefield, plus many more wounded who would die of their wounds in the days afterwards. The rebels had suffered an irreparable blow to their prestige (a quality that is of the utmost importance within Arab societies), and there were more defections to the government.

The SAS stepped up the civil aid projects and increased the military pressure on the *adoo*. By 1974 seven SAS teams, together with *firqats*, had cleared all the central valleys in central Dhofar. By the next year the rebels had been pushed back to the Yemeni border, and in December they had lost their last town in Dhofar. To all intents and purposes the war was won, and in September 1976 the SAS squadrons were withdrawn from Oman, signalling the successful conclusion of the campaign. However, in reality the SAS has never left Oman, for its men continue to train the SAF and hold training exercises in Oman itself. A grateful sultan is only too pleased to continue the ties with the UK and the SAS, and for its part the Regiment is more than happy to train its men in the demanding environment of the Gulf.

Oman is not the only Gulf country to which the SAS has access. Dubai, for example, a member of the United Arab Emirates, has close ties with the UK, and its Presidential Guard is led and trained by former SAS soldiers.

With its pedigree in desert warfare, allied to its close association with the armed forces and governments of several Gulf states, it was inevitable that the SAS would be deployed against the forces of Saddam Hussein. Therefore, as a force of more than half a million men was assembled by the Allies in Saudi Arabia, SAS units quietly made their way to the combat zone, to prepare once more to fight a desert war.

At the beginning of the 1990s, SAS soldiers were much fitter and better equipped than their World War II predecessors. They were also more 'rounded' soldiers in that they had more skills. They could handle four-wheel-drive desert vehicles with as much skill and dexterity as the 'Originals', but they were also trained in counter-terrorist tactics, small boat and canoe techniques, mountain warfare, and parachuting. Their equipment was also better: state-of-the-art communications kit, lighter weapons with more

Above: SAS soldiers and firqat members in Oman in the 1970s. These irregular units, raised and trained by the Regiment from Dhofaris, did not operate as conventional infantry, but as intelligence gatherers and reconnaissance troops.

firepower, and clothing that was able to withstand climate extremes. The modern Selection and Continuation courses has ensured that only the mentally and physically fittest get into the SAS. Just as well, for the Iraqis and the weather were going to put them to the ultimate test.

CHAPTER 2

Rehearsals for War

The seizure of the Western hostages by Saddam Hussein and their use as human shields necessitated the High Command in Riyadh putting together a plan for their rescue. The SAS and SBS, plus their American counterparts, were tasked with getting the hostages out alive, and each unit put together a rescue plan. However, Britain's élite warriors were very doubtful that it could be pulled off, and they knew the price in innocent blood would be high.

It was fortuitous, perhaps, that two squadrons of the SAS were already in the Arabian Gulf when Saddam Hussein's legions stormed into Kuwait, for the Allies could call upon the immediate services of a special forces unit well honed in desert warfare skills. D and G Squadrons were in Dhofar province, Oman, refining their desert warfare skills although, somewhat ironically, G Squadron was not employed during the actual conflict. As it became clear that the Iraqis would not push farther south into Saudi Arabia, the Regiment could assemble its men in the largest concentration of SAS troops since World War II.

The desert is one of the most inhospitable terrains in which any soldier can fight. The environment is subject to extremes of temperature, ranging from freezing cold at night to stiflingly hot during the day (though during the Gulf War SAS soldiers were subjected to freezing conditions during the day as well). To give some idea of the terrain in which the Regiment operated during the conflict, it is worth noting that Iraq covers an area of some 435,000 square kilometres (167,950 sq miles), and comprises 75 per cent desert, 13 per cent arable land, nine per cent meadow and three per cent forest. (Kuwait is almost entirely desert.) Missions in such areas are physi-

Opposite: General Norman Schwarzkopf, who was at first very sceptical about the employment of special forces in the Gulf.

Right: The aftermath of the Iraqi invasion of Kuwait – the empty streets and burnt-out buildings of Kuwait City. The 16,000-strong Kuwaiti Army was swept aside by Saddam's men.

cally demanding, with dehydration, sunstroke and sunburn all posing serious threats. High levels of physical fitness and stamina are a must, as is proper water discipline and personal hygiene. The latter is particularly important: intestinal diseases are a constant threat, and all team members have to constantly check each other for any signs of injury, however slight, because insects and dust can cause infection of minor cuts and scratches.

The desert is also hard on weapons and equipment, and SAS troops must ensure that hardware is constantly maintained. Too much oil applied to a rifle, for example, results in it mixing with sand and dust to form an abrasive paste that can damage the moving parts of the weapon. In addition, ammunition has to be kept out of the heat of the sun, and communications equipment can also suffer in the heat. All these things have to be taken into consideration by SAS teams in the desert. There is also the problem of camouflage. In the flat, featureless terrain of the desert the chances of a team being discovered are greatly increased. This is often underestimated by special forces teams, and discovery by keen-eyed locals was a problem for both the British and Americans throughout the Gulf War. As will be shown below, the SAS certainly possessed the skills for desert warfare, but would it have the manpower?

In August 1990, 22 Special Air Service Regiment consisted of four so-called 'Sabre' (fighting) squadrons – A, B, D and G – plus a reserve, R Squadron. Each SAS squadron consists of four 16-man troops, and each one has its own warfare speciality. Therefore there is a Mountain Troop which specialises in arctic and winter warfare, a Boat Troop that conducts amphibious warfare operations, a Mobility Troop which operates vehicles and motorcycles, and an Air Troop that specialises in airborne insertion techniques, specifically parachuting. The troops are further

divided into four four-man patrols, which can operate as independent units in wartime. Thus although the paper strength of a squadron is 64 men, squadrons are often below strength as a result of the exacting recruitment procedures that the Regiment operates. A cursory examination of the selection processes employed by the SAS will illustrate why this is the case.

To become an SAS soldier a serving member of Her Majesty's armed forces must volunteer himself. He will then be appointed to one of the Selection Training courses that are held twice each year. The course lasts for one month and consists of a three-week build-up period and Test Week. Selection consists of strenuous cross-country marches, which include map-reading

and navigation. The men are watched and their reactions assessed all the time as the distances they have to cover are increased, as is the weight they have to carry on their backs. The arduous Test Week decides who will go onto the next stage of SAS training: Continuation. The drop-out and failure rate on Selection is phenomenal, and by the end of the course between 90 and 95 per cent of volunteers will have returned to their original units.

The next stage of training is Continuation, in the course of which the prospective SAS soldier learns basic SAS skills. The course, which is much more exacting than Selection, takes the men to the jungles of Brunei and Belize and gives them instruction in escape and evasion,

The squadrons themselves are supported by specialists from the British Army who provide a variety of military skills. They include the Royal Army Medical Corps, the Royal Signals and the Royal Electrical and Mechanical Engineers. The men from these units are allowed to wear the beige SAS beret, but they wear the cap badges of their parent unit not the famous Winged Dagger.

When the invasion of Kuwait took place in August 1990, SAS soldiers were scattered far and wide, some in Northern Ireland combating the terrorist threat, others on secondment to friendly nations undertaking liaison and training duties. Stirling Lines, the location at Hereford of the SAS's headquarters, had to assemble its men for the trip to Saudi Arabia. As mentioned above, D and G Squadrons were already in theatre, but the other squadrons had to be recalled from their assignments. This was done in some haste, although it would in fact be many months before the operation to free Kuwait would occur. A member of B Squadron remembers the excitement the men felt at the time:

'The day Iraq invaded Kuwait we were travelling back from an intelligence briefing over the water [Northern Ireland] and were convinced that by the time we got to Hereford the rest of our squadron would have packed and left for Saudi without us.'

The general feeling among those members of the Regiment who were not already in Saudi Arabia was that they would 'miss the action'. Another SAS soldier who was serving in Ulster

survival techniques and parachuting skills. If, after having passed successfully all the hurdles of training, the recruit becomes a fully 'badged' member of the SAS. He is assigned to one of the four Sabre squadrons, but he is regarded very much as a fledgling SAS trooper who has yet to learn his trade (in his career with the Regiment he will be continually learning new skills).

at the time hurried back to the UK with his fellow patrol members:

'There was a direct flight to Birmingham from Belfast harbour, which was useful as it was nearer Hereford and saved travelling time at the other end. However, the flight was full so we legged it to Aldegrove and caught the London flight. It was pissing down when we landed at Heathrow. Typical. As soon as we left the aircraft I got an *Evening Standard* [newspaper] to see what the Government's reaction was to the Iraqi invasion. We were all confident that within days we would be moving to Saudi, even if only to a stand-off position.'

This general consensus was correct, for there was an urgent mission for the SAS and American special forces to fulfil: the rescue of Western hostages being held by Saddam Hussein. On 19 August, the Iraqi dictator had sent an open letter to the families of Westerners in Iraq, in which he expressed his anguish at the decision of the Iraqi National Assembly, i.e. himself, to detain their family members in Iraq. He stated that they would be released immediately once all Western forces had left Saudi Arabia, leaving the Arabs alone to settle the question of Kuwait. Not unnaturally, the British and American Governments refused this 'offer'. Instead, they began formulating plans for the rescue of the hostages by their special forces.

On the British side, the prospect facing the SAS was daunting. Lieutenant-General Peter de la Billière, the commander of the British forces in the Gulf, had tasked the Regiment to consider ways of getting the hostages out alive. None of the Allied commanders based in Riyadh wanted to be responsible for killing the hostages when the war started, i.e. killed by bombs dropped

from Allied aircraft. There were approximately 1000 British citizens in Iraq when the invasion occurred, with a further 800 trapped in Kuwait when the Iraqis rolled into the country. The SAS was not alone in its task. Air Chief Marshal Paddy Hine, for example, the Joint Commander of Operation 'Granby' (the codename for the overall British effort in the Gulf), set up a planning team at RAF High Wycombe, headquarters of RAF Strike Command, to devise ways of getting the hostages out. In addition, the planners in the UK kept in close contact with the Foreign Office, who in turn used the BBC World Service to transmit messages to the hostages from friends and relations. In this way, it was hoped, at least the morale of the hostages in general would be maintained while the British and Americans thought up ways to get them out.

Meanwhile, back in England, the Regiment was beginning to ship its soldiers to the Middle East. Those officers and men of D and G Squadrons who were still in the UK were quickly flown out to Saudi Arabia. For those left behind, and seemingly about to miss the action, this period was a time of intense frustration:

For those soldiers still stuck at Hereford, the weeks after the invasion passed slowly

---

'When we arrived back at our squadron lines rumour control was in overdrive. It was like buzz city; everyone had their theory on when we would be going and what we would be doing. But at the end of the day we learnt the squadron wasn't going anywhere, at least not immediately. The following Monday, though, the programme was rescheduled and we found

ourselves attending a series of briefings about the situation inside Iraq and the overall capability of Saddam's forces, which had been carefully collated by military intelligence.'

The SAS has its own intelligence cell at Stirling Lines. Called the Operations and Planning cell, it is nicknamed the 'Kremlin' as a throwback to the days of the Cold War. It holds detailed information on every prospective theatre of operations in which SAS soldiers may find themselves. As

Above: American reinforcements board a Boeing 747 airliner prior to flying to the Middle East. Among the American special forces units sent to the Gulf were US Navy SEALs and the 5th Special Forces Group.

the Regiment boasts it can send its members anywhere in the world at a moment's notice, one can imagine the amount of information that is stored there. In truth it is an invaluable part of any SAS mission, for when a team is despatched to a foreign country, it will be briefed on that country's climate, geography, political situation, social and economic conditions, and anything else that is pertinent to its mission.

For those soldiers still stuck at Hereford, the weeks after the August invasion of Kuwait passed slowly, as a member of B Squadron relates:

'A lot of my squadron were still away on courses, others were away working in training teams,

Below: British troops practice desert warfare NBC drills in Saudi in late 1990. Iraq had a large chemical and biological arsenal, and the Coalition's troops, the SAS included, were dreading having to fight in 'noddy' suits.

as well as being ready to provide support to the regimental staff serving in Ulster. I just hoped that if the balloon went up I wasn't going to be stuck in that shithole.'

The above view about service in Northern Ireland is widespread in the Regiment, a far cry from the public perception. Another SAS soldier explains why:

'The bloody rules and regulations are so tight over there these days it's ridiculous. You need to make sure that before you slot a Provo he has an Armalite muzzle stuck in your face and has IRA written on his balaclava; if he shoots at you that's even better!'

As August, September and October passed, giving way to November, those men who had passed Selection in August 1990, and had also completed Continuation, began to filter back to the Regiment. They were now 'badged' and could be sent out to the Middle East, after having been assigned to their squadrons first. Five teams from B Squadron were sent out in November, though not the full squadron, to boost manpower levels on the ground in Saudi Arabia. Before they went they were issued with equipment they would need to fight in the desert:

'Chukka [desert] boots were the order of the day, but I also packed a pair of US Marine jungle boots, which had steel plates in the sole but a breathable fabric around the ankle and leg. They would be ideal for the heat and the tough terrain. A combination of desert and cold weather kit was essential as it can get very cold at night. I also packed a roll-neck jumper which I had "liberated" from a mate, as well as gloves, woolly hat and thermal socks.'

The Iraqi dictator exhorted terrorist organisations to wreak havoc

Another who went out at this time provides the general Special Air Service philosophy on clothing for foreign assignments:

'At the end of the day it's all a case of being comfortable without being too overloaded, and everyone in the Regiment has their favourite item of clothing, be it a pair of gloves, a hat or a special flying jacket that they have "borrowed" from some senior RAF officer.'

Despite the fact that everyone at Hereford was 'booted and spurred ready to go', there were

Above: Saddam Hussein's television broadcast with some of the Western hostages endeavoured to show a benevolent leader. The reality was that the hostages were later scattered far and wide at strategic points – and the SAS had to find them.

some very good reasons for delaying their departure. First, the planning and preparation in the UK included a vast amount of refresher training for situations that could develop in the months ahead. This naturally took time as men were processed through these courses. Second, and just as important, there was the terrorist threat. All squadrons are rotated through counter-terrorist training at Hereford, and at any one time there is a squadron on 24-hour standby for anti-terrorist and hostage-rescue operations. As Iraq had been adjudged guilty by the West of state-sponsored terrorism, and as it was thought Saddam would use terrorism as a way of hitting back at Allied member states, it was obviously prudent to guard against this (the Iraqi dictator exhorted terrorist organisations to wreak havoc on his behalf; for example, on 27 January 1991 the Iraqi

SAS GULF WARRIORS

Right: The wreckage of a British Airways Boeing 747 at Kuwait City's airport. The threat of terrorist attacks, on Hussein's orders, against airliners at British airports meant the SAS had to intensify its aircraft assault training. Fortunately, this scenario did not become a reality.

Revolutionary Command Council stated that 'any Iraqi, Arab or Muslim taking part in a commando attack against the nations participating in the barbaric aggression against Iraq, their interests or their allies, will be considered a martyr in the "Mother of All Battles"'). Therefore, the counter-terrorist teams were on red alert – the threat of an Iraqi unit hijacking an aircraft in the UK was considered to be very high. The SAS counter-terrorist teams had worked out their strategy: 'There are several air bases we train at, but intelligence had indicated that the PLO [Palestine Liberation Organisation] could also hit an aircraft to highlight their support for Iraq, and it was believed by the SAS that they would try and torch the aircraft to gain maximum PR impact of an exploding ball of fire at Heathrow, in the heart of the British capital.'

The Regiment put its aircraft hostage-rescue drills into overdrive, but at the back of the men's minds were doubts:

'The concept of trying to rescue passengers as their kidnappers let off incendiary devices inside the aircraft sent a shiver down our spines. On a more practical level, it caused us to reassess our plans to access a hijacked aircraft in such a dangerous scenario. At one stage we were training in heavy flameproof suits with fire extinguishers strapped to the back of each man. After the first team had stormed the aircraft and put down a stun grenade [a small, non-lethal device that produces a loud bang and blinding flash when the ring is pulled – ideal for disorientating terrorists immediately prior to an assault], the follow-up team would rip the extinguishers off their backs and tackle the fire.

'I for one was glad the situation never arose, because the minute the front aircraft door opens the wind just feeds any fire and an incendiary can ignite a very large area in seconds. The fumes would be killing people before we had a chance to get into the aircraft and get them out.'

Although there would not be a terrorist atrocity on the British mainland during the Gulf conflict, the threat never subsided and SAS manpower had to be assigned to cover that threat. For those who were leaving for Saudi Arabia, however, it was time to say their goodbyes to friends and family. As ever, men took their leave of the UK in different ways. For those with wives and children, there was the usual heartache of saying farewell, not knowing when, or indeed

if, they would return. For those with no such ties the final days were very different:

'The weekend before we left, my mate and I went into Hereford for a quiet couple of sherbets. We hit the wine bar and then ended up in a nightclub, where we met some other blokes from the squadron and got absolutely shit-faced.'

'My mate's mum and dad lived in Birmingham and he wanted to see them before he left. So we drove down and opted to stay the night and

check out the nightlife of Brum, before we were going to be locked away in the desert with only a camel to bonk. We ended up with a couple of girls who worked in a bank, and they invited us back to their flat. When I discovered mine was from Dundalk, a breeding ground for IRA supporters, I laughed my head off. I bet she'd have a fit if she knew she had been fucked by a member of the SAS. I had been married myself, but my wife always wanted me to leave the forces. When I told her I was going on Selection she wasn't impressed, so I sacked her and we got divorced. My old man always told me that if it ain't broke don't fix it, but my marriage was broke big time.'

As always, those in the Regiment imparted as little information about their mission and destination as possible, as befits soldiers who operate out of the limelight:

'When we left for the Gulf I just telephoned my parents and told them I was off to the United States on exercise for a few weeks. My Dad knew what was going on, but I hoped my Mother didn't.'

'We spent the night exchanging ditts with mates already in theatre'

Their goodbyes all said, those remaining SAS soldiers who were to fly out to Saudi Arabia began the journey from RAF Lyneham, Wiltshire. The Regiment has use of a fleet of aircraft: Lockheed C-130 Hercules long-range transport aircraft courtesy of 47 Squadron based at Lyneham. And now these particular aircraft were working overtime to ferry the men and their equipment to the Middle East. As always, there were the inevitable bureaucratic procedures:

'As usual with Her Majesty's Royal Air Force, they wanted us to arrive at Lyneham the night before we flew out to the Middle East. So the 10 of us were dropped off in the early evening and booked into "Stalag Towers", a block of dreadful transit accommodation for military personnel flying out of Lyneham.'

The Hercules aircraft were drawn up in a long line on the tarmac, with engineers and mechanics working frantically to ensure all of them would be able to fly the next day. Security was tighter than usual, with RAF police patrols on Land Rovers driving up and down the base ensuring that no one had got in who was not supposed to be there. Lyneham was a hive of activity, as the aircraft were loaded with stores for the Gulf. For individual SAS soldiers, a long journey lay ahead:

'I remember smelling the distinctive aroma of aviation fuel. Anyone who has jumped from a Herc will know it: a sort of sweet paraffin. It can be quite nice, until you are standing hot and sweaty inside the aircraft waiting to jump, when a whiff of fuel suddenly sticks in your throat, making you throw up. Boarding a Herc at 0400 hours is never a popular move. Our kit had already been packed on a pallet and loaded, but I carried my doss bag [sleeping bag] with me, plus a book and a Walkman. It was going to be a long flight, and there was only one way to pass the time: sleep and dream. After a fuel stop in Cyprus it would be on to Saudi.

'All in all it had been 17 hours of travelling and everyone was looking forward to getting off the

Herc. The thump of the aircraft's wheels being lowered and the distinctive locking of the under-carriage is a firm sign that it is time to return to your seat and prepare for landing.'

The SAS soldiers were flown into Riyadh air base, from where they were taken in vehicles hired from the Saudi authorities to nearby bar-racks, where there were other soldiers from the Regiment:

'We spent the night exchanging ditts with mates already in theatre, and then crashed in our sleeping bags in readiness of an intense week of acclimatisation to the heat, as well as preparing our equipment.'

The SAS has a tried and tested method when it comes to camouflaging weapons and equipment: daub it in drab camouflage paint and, in the par-lance of the Regiment, 'make it look as shitty as possible'. At this time it was not only men who were being shipped out to the Middle East. Stores were being continually flown out from RAF Lyneham, including medical supplies, clothing, radio spares, plus each SAS squadron's general re-supply equipment.

The true nature of the Iraqi dictator was revealed towards the end of October

---

Soon there was an impressive British special for-ces contingent in the Gulf, consisting of 300 'badged' SAS soldiers (from A, B and D Squad-rons), 15 men from R Squadron, elements of the Special Boat Service (SBS), and RAF special forces aircrew. In all, there were 700 British spe-cial forces men ready to put in motion plans for rescuing the hostages held by the Iraqis. There was only one problem: where exactly were they?

In an effort to deter any Allied, specifically American, attacks upon Iraq, Saddam had dis-persed the hostages to many sites throughout Iraq and Kuwait to act as 'human shields'. This began on the night of 17/18 August 1990, when 35 Americans were despatched to several strate-gic sites. Though this was greeted with outrage in the West, Saddam played the hostage card very cleverly, and often diffused the world's anger. For example, he released 80 Austrians on 25 August, and three days later a further 3000 Western and Far Eastern hostages, comprising all the Western and Japanese women and children, were also given their freedom. Nevertheless, the true nature of the Iraqi dictator was revealed towards the end of October, when he had 661 of the hostages, including 260 Britons and 103 Americans, placed at economic and military sites as protection against Allied air attacks. In this way he hoped to gain time to build up Iraq's defences against the Allies, specifically its anti-aircraft capability (at this time he still had 3700 Western and Japanese hostages). In addition, the 26 staff of the US Embassy in Kuwait City itself were virtually under siege, and their supplies of food and water were running out.

Against this sombre background the British and American special forces made frantic efforts to formulate plans to get all the hostages out. All special forces operations in the Gulf were con-trolled by the Allied Special Operations Com-mand of Central Command (SOCCENT) in Riyadh, and it was through this organisation that the plans were made (all Coalition forces in the Gulf were directed by US Central Command (CENTCOM), under its Commanding General, General Norman Schwarzkopf). Despite the grandiose title, SOCCENT could not come up

Above: British troops on exercise in the Saudi desert. Even for professional soldiers, operating in such terrain is difficult enough. The SBS worked out prospective escape routes for rescued hostages across the desert.

with anything that inspired much confidence. For example, the commander of the SAS, Colonel Andrew Massey, consulted with Lieutenant-General Peter de la Billière about rescuing the hostages. Neither man was confident, as de la Billière later stated in his Gulf War memoirs: 'At no stage did I feel that we could have recovered more than half the Britons, if that.' As the Iraqis kept moving them from location to location, and in any case the Allies did not have reliable information about what locations were holding hostages, this seemed an accurate assessment. Typi-

cally, the appraisal of the situation by SAS soldiers themselves was more earthy:

'The biggest concern for the Regiment at this stage was how to rescue the hostages taken by Saddam. Quite frankly it was a fucking nightmare; no one seemed to know anything about them, apart from what we saw on CNN [Cable

Network News]. The questions that arise in such an operation are: are they moved to different locations every day, are the buildings booby-trapped, and how many access points are there? All these questions were unanswered. The only bit of intelligence we could get hold off were the CNN films that had been taken. We videoed these and watched them frame by frame.'

Nevertheless, the SAS was far from happy. It worked closely with the Americans in putting together a plan (an SAS captain had been assigned to the US Special Forces Command to work alongside the US 5th Special Forces Group, US Navy SEALs, Psyops and Civaid), though the end result was far from ideal. It was decided that a joint operation mounted with the Americans

machines flown by Chinook Squadron Middle East (a temporary unit made up of equipment and personnel from No.7 Squadron at Odiham in the UK and 18 Squadron at Gütersloh in Germany). The Chinook can carry up to 50 fully equipped troops, which meant there would not be enough fuselage space to evacuate the hostages. So the SAS looked to the Americans.

The US Special Operations command possessed helicopters that were ideally suite to clandestine infiltration, and could therefore be used for a hostage-rescue mission. The helicopters would come from three squadrons: the 20th, 21st and 55th Special Operations Squadrons. The 20th and 21st operated the very large Sikorsky MH-53J Sea Stallion 'Pave Low' helicopters, while the 55th flew the smaller Sikorsky MH-60G Black Hawk 'Pave Hawk' helicopter. Both types had been developed for special forces combat rescue missions, and were thus ideal for getting into and out of enemy-held territory. The 'Pave Low' version of the CH-53 is a formidable helicopter. Extremely fast, it has armour plate and 7.62mm Miniguns. Its other defensive measures include chaff dispensers and an advanced electronic countermeasures (ECM) system. Its navigational capabilities are also impressive: a terrain-following/terrain-avoidance radar combined with a forward-looking infrared (FLIR) system and pilot-worn night vision goggles. These helicopters are designed to carry nearly 40 fully equipped troops. For the rescue of the hostages, it was assumed that around double this

would offer the best chance of success. The Americans would mount a diversion while the SAS would undertake the rescue, using British and US helicopters.

From a logistical point of view, the use of American helicopters made sense. The only suitable British helicopters for such a mission were the 15 Boeing Vertol Chinook HC.Mk 1

number of civilians could be crammed into each fuselage at least.

There were, in addition, several more helicopters that the Allies possessed that could be an asset in a hostage-rescue mission. These were a number of Soviet-built Mil Mi-8 'Hip' helicopters that had arrived behind Coalition lines in the hands of defecting Iraqis. These helicopters were later used by US Special Forces in a raid to bring back sensitive frontline radar equipment in January 1991. However, it is possible that the same aircraft would have been used either to mount a distraction for the mission, or actually take part in the mission itself. The latter option, though, would depend on the availability of long-range fuel tanks for the helicopters: 'Hips' can usually transport up to 32 fully equipped troops; more kit-free civilians can obviously be accommodated, but the long-range fuel tanks would also take up valuable space.

After the SAS had located the hostages, the helicopters would be called in

---

How would the SAS conduct the actual rescue of the hostages? It is now clear that SAS teams would have made parachute drops at the many locations where it was believed the hostages were being held. The men would have made a High Altitude, Low Opening (HALO) drop onto the targets, thereby ensuring that they arrived silently and thus achieved maximum surprise: with a HALO descent the team leaves the aircraft at an altitude of around 10,000m (32,810ft) and deploys parachutes at around 760m (2500ft) so that the men land together and do not have to waste time looking for each

other. After the SAS had located the hostages, the helicopters would be called in to evacuate them. The plan was incredibly risky, and was made all the more so by several factors. First, the exact location of all the hostages was unknown because the Iraqis moved them from site to site. Second, the SAS teams would be assaulting heavily defended military sites, increasing the likelihood of both SAS and hostage casualties. Third, the SAS would not be able to call upon the support of helicopter and aircraft gunships to soften up the defences due to the risk to the hostages (though gunships would accompany the rescue helicopters for general suppression once the hostage had been evacuated). If the evacuation helicopters failed to arrive for any reason, the SBS had drawn up detailed emergency escape routes. However, the idea of hundreds of civilians tramping across the desert until they were picked up by fresh helicopters (see above for description of the terrain indigenous to Iraq and Kuwait), pursued by Iraqi soldiers, must have filled the planners with dread. As one SAS soldier said afterwards: 'I am sure it would have cost many lives.'

The fact that it was the British SAS which was to be the instrument for freeing the hostages raises serious questions about the USA's own hostage-rescue unit, Delta Force. The latter, closely modelled on the British SAS, was formed in 1977 and is responsible for foreign counter-terrorist operations which involve the capture of hostaged US personnel, installations or property. Its most famous, or infamous, operation since its creation had been the abortive rescue of American hostages being held in Tehran in 1980. Its reputation had not been enhanced during subsequent operations. The SAS was therefore very

Above: British armour on transports moves across the desert as preparations for Operation 'Desert Storm' begin in earnest. By the end of 1990 there were 35,000 British military personnel in the Gulf, including a special forces group numbering 700.

much the senior partner when it came to rescuing the hostages. That said, Delta Force was determined to prove itself in the Gulf, and had been selected for a high-profile mission: the rescue of the staff under virtual siege in the US Embassy in Kuwait City.

For months before the war began, the Americans had been working on plans to free the diplomats and staff trapped in the embassy. The final plan, codenamed Operation 'Pacific Wind', was typically American, i.e. complex. The mission involved 18 McDonnell Douglas F-15E Strike Eagle attack fighters, four Lockheed F-117 Night Hawk 'stealth' attack warplanes, four

Grumman F-14 Tomcat carrier-borne air-superiority fighters, and an assortment of Grumman A-6 Intruder carrier-borne attack and Grumman EA-6 Prowler carrier-borne electronic warfare aircraft, plus Delta Force personnel in helicopter transports.

The first part of the plan, to be launched at night, involved two F-117s bombing two power plants in Kuwait City to knock out all the lights in the city. Simultaneously, the other two F-117s would completely flatten a high-rise hotel located near the embassy complex. This would prevent the anti-aircraft guns positioned on the hotel's roof firing on Delta Force's helicopters, and would also kill all those Iraqi officers billeted in the hotel itself. The Prowlers would detect, classify and suppress enemy electronic activity in support of the air strikes, while the Intruders would aid the Eagles in bombing and strafing enemy gun pits along the beach near the embassy compound and three boulevards leading to the embassy itself. With the enemy's defences suppressed, Delta Force's helicopters would swoop in and evacuate the staff from the compound. To rehearse this complex rescue plan, a Delta Force squadron had secretly flown to Nevada to practice operating in the desert, while others rehearsed hostage-rescue drills at Fort Bragg. And in Florida, at Hurlburt Field, F-15 crews practised the sort of precision air-to-ground strikes that would be needed if the operation was going to succeed.

As the British and American élite prepared their effort to pull off the nearly impossible, Saddam decided to release the hostages in a move that included the peaceful evacuation of the embassy in Kuwait City. In typical fashion, the Iraqi dictator had decided that he had milked the hostages for all they were worth in terms of influencing world opinion. On 18 November

1990, therefore, Iraq announced that it had authorised the 'foreign guests' to start leaving from 25 December onwards, with the last departure being on 25 March 1991, providing 'nothing comes to disturb the climate of peace'. In fact, on 6 December 1990 he would authorise the immediate release of all the hostages. The SAS soldiers, and no doubt those from Delta Force, breathed a huge collective sigh of relief. A potentially bloody operation had been avoided, and the Allied special forces were free to concentrate on other objectives. But as 1990 drew to a close and the Allied build-up continued, the soldiers of the British Special Air Service were left to ponder one unanswered question: what exactly would they do now?

CHAPTER 3

Plan of Campaign

The beginning of 1991 was a period of uncertainty for the SAS in the Gulf. The Western hostages had been freed from Saddam's clutches. But what task was there now for the Regiment? The SAS was but one of many special forces units deployed to the Gulf, and it looked as though it would have no part in the overall plan of campaign. However, by the middle of January things began to change: and now it would be given the opportunity to fight its desert war.

With the release of the hostages who had been held by Saddam Hussein, the Special Air Service was without a specific mission. This was not at first appreciated by the SAS men themselves, or by their commanders in Riyadh. The immediate thoughts of the latter that they could concentrate on conducting the kind of desert war that David Stirling had waged 50 years earlier, i.e. hit-and-run missions behind the lines. This in itself seemed appropriate enough, though the Regiment faced two obstacles to its further involvement in the Gulf War.

First, and most importantly, was the hostility of General Norman Schwarzkopf towards special forces operations in general. Nicknamed the 'Bear', and with a temper like one with a sore head, Schwarzkopf had definite views on the capabilities and shortcomings of elite units. In short, he was a sceptic when it came to unconventional warfare. As a Vietnam War veteran, he had seen many special forces missions go wrong. He had also seen how clandestine operations had absorbed conventional assets when they went wrong. As he said before the Gulf War broke out: 'When you go to war, you're going to war all the way. That's exactly where I come from. No more Cambodian border situations for me.' Above all,

Opposite: Some of the 20,000 Syrian troops sent to Saudi Arabia to support the UN effort. Schwarzkopf was unsure as to the enthusiasm of some of the Arab contingents, and so he used the American Green Berets as eyes and ears on the ground to assess their morale.

SAS GULF WARRIORS

Above: Lieutenant-General de la Billière, the commander of the British forces in the Gulf, would not sanction the use of the SAS in the war unless he believed there was a worthwhile task for the Regiment to fulfil.

Schwarzkopf was determined that special forces operations would not affect adversely his plans for the overall direction and conduct of the campaign against Iraqi forces. This being so, it was highly unlikely that he would sanction the kind of campaign waged by David Stirling in the Western Desert in World War II. Above all, he wanted the Gulf War to be tightly controlled.

The enemy was to be methodically worn down and destroyed, first by an intensive air campaign, then by a ground offensive. There would therefore be little scope for what he saw as 'wild cat' special forces missions.

The second obstacle to further SAS involvement was, surprisingly, an ex-commander of the SAS: Lieutenant-General Peter de la Billière. Once the Western hostages had been freed, he was determined that the SAS should take part in hostilities only if two conditions regarding its use were fulfilled: first that there was a worthwhile function for the SAS to perform; and second that there must be the means to extract SAS teams in emergency situations. As 1990 drew to a close, neither condition had been fulfilled. In fact, one of the largest wars involving British forces since Korea was about to begin and the UK's best soldiers did not have a role.

The first thing they did was to fully acclimatise themselves and their equipment

The SAS soldiers themselves did not initially worry about such trivialities. The first thing they did was to fully acclimatise themselves and their equipment to their new theatre of operations. The men trained to fight a highly mobile campaign, as a member of D Squadron relates:

'Mobility was regarded as the key to success for the Regiment if it was to be called upon to mount cross-border attacks into Iraq. Therefore, the RAF's No.7 Special Forces Flight, based at Odiham in Hampshire, would play a crucial role in this area of operation.'

The Boeing Vertol Chinook helicopters from Odiham were already in the theatre and were

being painted and kitted out for clandestine insertions into enemy territory. In addition, the Regiment's whole fleet of Land Rover 110s, nicknamed 'Pinkies', were also on their way to the Middle East, and they were supplemented by the delivery of a further 20 Land Rover 90s. These diesel-engined vehicles were smaller than the 110s, and quickly became known as 'Din-kies' because of this fact.

As a bonus with regard to mobility, before the Iraqi invasion of Kuwait the Regiment had been testing a new type of vehicle in Oman. This was called the Light Strike Vehicle (LSV), and the

Above: British troops in northwest Saudi Arabia, near the SAS's forward operating base. Note the terrain, in which the men of the Regiment would have to construct observation posts to observe enemy movements.

vehicles of this type had been supplied by Longline Ltd, a Sussex-based company that had designed them specially for the Regiment's use (the concern is now called Cobra Longline Defence). They resembled the dune buggies that the US Special Forces were already using, and were described by SAS men themselves as look-ing 'like something out of a Mad Max movie'.

The LSVs were just one item of equipment that was being tested in Oman in the spring and summer of 1990, for the SAS is in an enviable position with regard to equipment procurement, as a serving member explains: 'Over a decade after the Falklands War the budget for weapons and equipment has soared, and within reason anything that is of interest to the Regiment's procurement team is allocated funding.' In the event, the LSVs were not used in conflict, except for border reconnaissance.

As is usual with the SAS, weapons and equipment are often modified to cater for specific missions, and so it was with the Land Rovers. The Land Rover 90s were fitted with a large metal rack across the front of the bonnet and a base plate fitted on the back. The idea of the latter was to fire a mortar from the rear of the vehicle. However, it was soon realised that the firing of such a weapon might collapse the vehicle's springs, so the idea was scrapped.

The Regiment had established a forward operating base in Saudi Arabia

By mid-December 1990, the Regiment was still rehearsing for a number of scenarios and missions, but nothing definite had been decided. The men themselves started to get bored and restless. The Regiment had established a forward operating base (FOB) in Saudi Arabia in August, but conditions there or at the air bases in theatre were hardly luxurious:

'Our accommodation was Spartan to say the least. We had taken over some offices on the southern side of the air base, and were living two or four to a room, as space would allow. Those who had flown in from Oman and had been first on the scene made sure that a television and all the domestic requirements had been procured, by one means or another.' As the High Command in Riyadh laid the finishing touches to its plans, the SAS waited.

At this point it would be useful to discuss the Iraqi test-firing of the Scud missile that took place at the beginning of December. Although the SAS's adventures with regard to the hunt for Scud missiles are told in a later chapter, it is relevant here to discuss the Scud threat. The Iraqis had test-fired three Scud missiles in western Iraq on 2 December 1990, a date which was subsequently termed 'Scud Sunday'. It has, in view of what later occurred in the war in relation to strikes upon Israel, assumed a magnitude that was not shared by the Allies at the time. That Iraq possessed such weapons capable of carrying a chemical or biological warhead was well known. However, before hostilities began it was believed that Allied aircraft, backed by satellite and AWACS aircraft, could pinpoint and destroy all Scud launch sites before Saddam could wreak a modern-day plague upon the Coalition forces. US Airborne Warning And Control System (AWACS) aircraft combine a large surveillance radar capable of detecting, identifying and tracking large numbers of aircraft at ranges exceeding several hundred kilometres. The onboard command and control facilities also mean that AWACS aircraft can direct fighters and other friendly aircraft. Only when the war broke out was this assumption proved false. At the begin-

Right: Part of the British 1st Armoured Division deployed in Saudi Arabia. Schwarzkopf was determined that his conventional units would take precedence over special forces in the Gulf.

sanctioned the flight back to the UK of the majority of those SAS soldiers in Saudi Arabia. As the men set off on the long flight home, each of them knew 'in the back of our minds that DLB [de la Billière] would do his best to use the Regiment's resources as best he could.' The men flew into RAF Brize Norton and the greyness of England, and then travelled straight to their families. This period of leave was strange, though, as a member of B Squadron remembers:

'On the day I arrived back I was with my mate and his family. It was great to be back, but both he and I were switching the tele on all the time to keep tabs on developments in the Gulf.'

As is usual in situations such as these, no one is allowed to be more than two hours travelling time from Hereford. This is a vital procedure, and ensures that troops and squadrons can move at short notice. Though it is sensible, it makes the men feel very restricted and thus prevents them mentally unwinding. Christmas was a difficult time for the men and their families, each side knowing that the recall could come at a moment's notice. When the order to move did come through, even the most hardened of the Regiment were choked with emotion. The following is an account of just one farewell, but in its own way is representative of them all:

'On the Friday evening I was eating my scoff [food] when my oppo came over to the table and said: "Word is we're off next week." I knew it would be a wrench for Scouse. He has three little girls and for the best part of 1990 he had been

ning of December 1990, though, everyone had faith in the airborne answer to the Scuds. Regarding the SAS, it did not feature in plans for the eradication of the Scud menace.

As Christmas approached the men naturally thought about home and loved ones. As the festive season got nearer the Regiment's top brass away on detachment, and another departure was not going to help the family. But his wife was a brick and would make sure that the family stood behind him.

'He didn't want his wife and kids coming up to the camp, so I said I would drive him down and pick him up. I arrived at the house just after 1800 hours, and had a cup of tea with the kids while Scouse went through a checklist of domestic "do-its" with his wife. The insurance was due on the car, and one of the tyres needed replacing. He didn't need to tell his wife as she always kept a tight rein on all the bills and the car, but I think it made him feel good to talk it through with

her. I said cheerio to the kids and went and sat in the car. Scouse followed me seconds later, throwing a holdall in the back of the car. He looked depressed and pale. As we drove towards Stirling Lines neither of us spoke, the silence was oppressive. Eventually he muttered quietly: "Thank fuck that's over, I fuckin' hate good-byes." I parked the car and handed the keys into

Below: Egyptian Rangers training for 'Desert Storm'. Despite his suspicions regarding special forces units, Schwarzkopf relied on his Green Berets to act as advisors and liaisers with the various national units under his command. He would also come to rely on the SAS in Iraq.

the guard room, then we both walked towards the accommodation block to collect our kit.'

The trip back to Saudi Arabia was made as comfortable as possible. Flasks of hot tea were packed for the trip to Brize Norton, and the men were, where possible, allocated to so-called 'comfort flights' aboard BAe VC10 transports of the Royal Air Force. The aircraft flew via Cyprus straight to Saudi Arabia, to King Khalid Military City, 400km (250 miles) from Riyadh:

PLAN OF CAMPAIGN

Left: An MH-53 'Pave Low' helicopter of the US Air Force's 20th Special Operations Squadron in the Gulf, which supported US élite units. Helicopters were invaluable for inserting and extracting special forces teams in the Gulf.

immediate operation to kick Saddam Hussein's hordes out of Kuwait.'

As the new year began, the SAS prepared for the kind of war its members believed they would fight. This involved sharpening up on observation post (OP) skills. The exact wartime role of the SAS is often misunderstood, though it has remained essentially unchanged since World War II. The Regiment is a long-range reconnaissance unit, whose members are trained to operate behind the lines in small groups. From hidden OPs deep inside enemy territory, SAS patrols are trained to send back intelligence concerning enemy strengths and dispositions to friendly headquarters. In this way, a small unit can have a war-winning potential. Although no one knew for sure what they would be doing once war broke out in the Gulf, 'buzz control' was alive with speculation, the most plausible being that the SAS would spend the war undertaking surveillance work.

'We attempted to get our "termite heads" on and dig into the hard terrain'

OP work is difficult and dangerous, and it was made the more so by the peculiarities of the terrain in which the men were operating. A member of A Squadron takes up the story:

'Packed like mules with scopes and night vision optics, we were inserted almost on the border line [the Saudi-Iraq border]. We attempt-

'It's a remote training base in the middle of the Saudi desert, and gave us protection from the prying eyes of the media and from other military agencies, and allowed us to prepare ourselves for what everyone presumed would be an almost

Above: Training for when the balloon goes up. By the middle of January 1991 the men of the Regiment believed that they would be undertaking surveillance work inside enemy territory to gather intelligence concerning Iraqi movements.

ed to get our "termite heads" on and dig into the hard terrain to get out of sight and out of danger from the sun, but the ground was rock-hard. Like all OP work, the priority was to establish a safe routine in which one man rests and one man works through the day, then vice versa at night. This ensures that there is a pair of eyes at all times. It was a "bare arse" position to insert into,

though, and we had therefore opted to get into undulating terrain which might afford us some protection. As is standard operating procedure (SOP), a second team of two was dug-in on some high ground behind us, from where they could provide protection in case we were "bumped".'

The men at the FOB were itching to cross the border and get closer to the Iraqi MSR (Main Supply Route) in western Iraq to check the strength of the enemy's convoys that were being used to pour supplies into occupied Kuwait.

The tactic of 'hit and run' to destroy Iraqi morale had been ruled out

---

However, at this stage the SAS was very much under tight control, and that control was American. The tactic of 'hit and run' to destroy Iraqi morale had been ruled out by Schwarzkopf, who was determined that the job of reducing the enemy's morale was given over to the fighters, bombers and ground-attack aircraft of the UN air fleets. Officially the Regiment went along with this, but privately the men and commanders of the SAS were 'particularly angered at Schwarzkopf's narrow viewpoint'. Specifically, they thought they were being punished for Delta Force's debacle at Desert One 10 years before, when America's hostage-rescue unit had failed ignominiously to rescue the hostages being held by militants in Tehran. In fact, the air campaign that preceded the ground offensive would effectively destroy the morale of most of the Iraqi divisions in Kuwait and southern and western Iraq. Allied special forces never got a chance to try their hand at demoralising the enemy, the nearest they got being dropping leaflets on the positions of enemy soldiers.

Despite their disappointment, the men continued to prepare. The day-to-day routine consisted of hard training during the morning and out of the sun in the afternoon attending briefing sessions. During these meetings personnel from the Intelligence Corps, affectionately known in the Regiment as the 'Green Slime', would provide detailed briefings on everything from Iraqi lifestyles and the terrain of the country to the morale of the enemy: in short, anything that would be essential to the battle plans. Aerial photographs were collected of Iraqi territory and passed on to the Regiment, plus information on all potential threats. The Intelligence Corps also provided a continuous stream of videos for the men to watch, which illustrated the Iraqi military in action during the eight-year war between Iran and Iraq. In this way the 'big picture' was soon completed.

However, it soon became clear that there was a gap in the intelligence: no one knew anything about Iraq's special forces. The only information available on them was that they appeared to be well-trained and equipped. All this information was presented on a massive model known to everyone as the 'bird table'. It contained sensitive details about Allied formations and, more importantly, indicated the potential areas of the desert where the 'Green Slime' believed the Scuds were sited or operated. 'The "bird table" was top secret. It was constantly updated and gave both our commanders and the intelligence boys a constant source of information concerning both friendly forces on the ground and enemy threats. The system is used by both brigade and divisional commanders and is regarded as being old fash-

ioned because it is manually operated. From our point of view all we were interested in were the "show stoppers". Difficult terrain, rivers and roads were to be avoided, plus any problems or hazards that were marked on the "bird table" which could cause grief to either a mobile or a foot patrol.'

While intelligence was being amassed concerning the Iraqis, another intelligence game was going on along the border. Coalition signals units – forward warfare teams – recorded allied radio transmissions during exercises that took place in the desert. This would form part of a massive deception plan. When the ground campaign to free Kuwait started, the signals teams broadcast these old tapes, thus giving the impression to the Iraqis that the Coalition forces were still stationed in their original positions. It was an excellent deception plan and one which undoubtedly helped the ground war.

Though they may be the West's crack troops, SAS soldiers are also very human, and they all felt the isolation as they trained for their forthcoming desert war:

'It's a strange feeling when you cannot communicate with home'

'None of us could 'phone home. We were in the middle of nowhere and no one, not even our own forces, was supposed to know where we were. Letters were allowed but they all went via the Ministry of Defence, who censored them.' Some felt the isolation more than others: 'It's a strange feeling when you cannot communicate with home; you can easily feel totally cut off from the rest of the world.'

Right: British Land Rover 110s in Saudi. All the Regiment's Land Rovers were shipped out to the Gulf in preparation for hostilities, with an additional 20 Land Rover 90s also provided for SAS use. The Land Rovers would provide sterling service behind Iraqi lines.

Such restrictions on communicating naturally affected the married men more than those who were single. Fortunately, within the Regiment there is a very strong wives' club, and whenever there are deployments abroad this group forms a solid emotional bulwark for those whose husbands are away. It is an essential part of the regimental family.

Waiting can breed boredom and frustration, and so the squadron and troop commanders ensured that everyone was kept as busy as possible. Reconnaissance patrols were mounted along the border and SAS vehicles provided escorts for convoys. While this was going on the Coalition was assembling its forces for the eventual liberation of Kuwait. The SAS soldiers were left in no doubt that they were but small cogs in a very large machine:

'Aboard a Land Rover 90 we shadowed a supply convoy during a short desert move. I was amazed. Until that point I had never seen so many vehicles. The logistics involved must have been a nightmare. As far as the eye could see there were Land Rovers and four-ton trucks.'

Early January 1991 seemed to be the nadir of fortune as far as the SAS was concerned. On 2 January de la Billière had been informed that Wing Commander David Farquhar, the Personal Staff Officer to Paddy Hine, had lost some secret documents and a lap-top computer that contained outline plans of the American war plan in the Gulf. Worse, news of the loss was heard not through official channels but via the BBC. Fortunately, both the papers and computer were later recovered, but de la Billière was faced with the awkward position of having to tell Schwarz-kopf. The latter seemed to take it in his stride, but the Americans were quite rightly dubious about further entrusting the British with classi-

fied information, and it cast British security in a bad light. While not directly affecting the SAS, it could have done the Regiment no good with regard to persuading Schwarzkopf that it deserved a place in the war. The views of the Regiment's soldiers themselves on the incident are typically succinct:

'The general comment of the day was "fucking wankers". He hadn't even got his desert boots on yet he'd compromised the entire plan for the British phase of the operation. Luckily, some decent bastard found it and handed it in. But it was too late by then. Whatever the plan had been, the top brass in Whitehall had already shit

Above: The Americans also brought their vehicles. This is a Chenworth Fast Attack Vehicle, several of which were used by Delta Force around Al Qaim. Dune buggies are fast and highly manoeuvrable, but have severe range limitations.

themselves and changed the orders – whatever they were it will be years before the details are released.'

At the end of the first week of January, the SAS was still unsure as to its role in the war. The previous month de la Billière had ordered the Regiment to prepare for missions deep inside Iraq. The SAS had expanded this to cover three main aspects: deep penetration missions into Iraq, mobile patrols and road watches along the MSRs. 'All we wanted was the green light to get going and do the business.' However, the Regiment was not going anywhere. Border recon-

naissance was still under the control of the US 5th Special Forces Group and the US Marine Corps' reconnaissance units. The specific roles of these organisations and where they fitted into the overall campaign plans is discussed below. For the moment, however, the American special forces held the upper hand.

The middle of January brought a revival in the Regiment's fortunes as de la Billière identified what he believed was a worthwhile task for the SAS. The Regiment would be detailed to create diversions and cut roads in western Iraq to draw away Iraqi forces from the front. This would also create fear and uncertainty in the minds of the enemy, who would, it was hoped, believe that a major operation was developing on his right flank. For a secondary role, de la Billière also believed that the SAS could attack Scud missile launchers, although at this stage the urgency of this task was not great. The SAS, excited at the prospect of at last having a real role, put on a briefing regarding its capabilities and objectives for General Schwarzkopf, who was so impressed that he sanctioned de la Billière's plans. He had been won over

Therefore, at last, the SAS stood poised to take an active part in the Gulf War. Yet it was just one of the special forces units deployed to Saudi Arabia, and by no means the largest. Typically, it was the Americans who had the greatest number of special forces in the Gulf.

The largest special forces contingent was the US 5th Special Forces Group, whose talents were sorely needed. In particular, the Arab forces in the Coalition had no experience of working in a multi-national military formation. Thus the Egyptians, Saudis, Syrians and others had different organisational and procedural methods, to say nothing of their equipment differences. They had to be welded together into an effective allied military machine. The best equipped to do this were the Green Berets, who are trained to organise and train foreign irregular units. This involves learning foreign customs, languages and cultures. In this they are like the SAS, whose 'hearts and minds' strategy is similar in content (see Chapter One). Therefore, Schwarzkopf called in the 5th Special Forces Group from Fort Campbell, Kentucky.

The men arrived on 5 September 1990, and faced their first task: to provide liaison with Saudi Arabian army units and undertake internal defence duties with them. A second, and more important, mission was to provide Schwarzkopf with intelligence concerning what was happening along the Saudi border. This meant that

Green Beret teams were themselves undertaking reconnaissance missions along the border. By November there were six Green Beret A Teams, backed up by Saudi paratroopers, in nine border posts along the border. As more and more units poured into Saudi Arabia, Schwarzkopf switched the emphasis of the 5th Special Forces Group to another urgent task: the reconstruction of the Kuwaiti Army. This was a daunting mission. Never large even before the Iraqi invasion – its strength was 16,000 men in five mechanised brigades – only one unit escaped to Saudi Arabia. It was duly reconstructed as an armoured brigade and equipped with Yugoslav T-84 tanks. The soldiers who trained the Kuwaitis were the Green Berets, and the latter were also instrumental in turning an assortment of Kuwaiti soldiers, students, refugees and expatriates into five Kuwaiti light infantry brigades. These units were obviously not at the same level of combat readiness as the units of the rest of the Coalition, but they were invaluable when it came to Arab morale and as part of those Arab forces that eventually liberated Kuwait City.

The fledgling Kuwaiti Army had no non-commissioned officers (NCOs)

Although they are first and foremost trainers, the US Special Forces encountered particular difficulties when it came to training and equipping the Kuwaiti units. The matériel was not such a problem, but the organisation of individual formations presented many problems. For example, the fledgling Kuwaiti Army had no non-commissioned officers (NCOs) and its officers were of rather dubious quality: in particular, because of the hierarchical nature of Kuwaiti society, the officers showed no inclination to undertake NCO-type duties. All leadership and knowledge therefore had to come from the American Green Beret advisors.

While this was going on, other Special Forces teams were deployed in an advisory capacity throughout the Allied Arab armies. This was not just for liaison purposes, important though this undoubtedly was, but also to provide General Schwarzkopf with accurate intelligence regarding general Arab morale and enthusiasm for the forthcoming war. In total there were 106 Green Berets teams among the Arab coalition forces. Their success may be judged by the effectiveness of the ground offensive in February 1991.

Other US Special Forces missions included deep reconnaissances conducted on behalf of the US 3rd Army. These teams operated some 200km (125 miles) into Iraqi-occupied territory, keeping watch on enemy reserve units, the élite Republican Guard and the main roads between Iraq and Kuwait. In this they were to perform many of the same tasks undertaken by the SAS in western Iraq (these are discussed in greater detail in later chapters).

The US SEALs established a Naval Special Warfare Task Group at Ras al Ghar

Mention has already been made of some of the US Air Force (USAF) squadrons that were deployed to the Gulf region. The 8th and 20th Special Operations Squadrons (flying MC-130 'Combat Talon' fixed-wing aircraft and MH-53 'Pave Low' helicopters respectively) were deployed soon after the Iraqi invasion of Kuwait,

Right: When they went into Iraq, the SAS vehicle columns were accompanied by motorcycle outriders, such as the one shown here. The bikes could carry out reconnaissance duties, but their fuel had to be carried by the Land Rovers.

closely followed by the 21st Special Operations Squadron. These USAF units conducted many missions during the war, including search and rescue and destroying enemy radar and communications sites. These missions were conducted after the air war had started. Four 'Pave Lows' were the spearhead for US Army McDonnell Douglas AH-64 Apache helicopters which opened up an air corridor for Coalition aircraft on the first night of the air war.

The US Navy's special forces units, the Sea-Air-Land (SEAL) teams, were ordered to begin preparing to move to Saudi Arabia on 7 August 1990. Within days all the weapons and equipment for Naval Special Warfare Group 1 was aboard Lockheed C-5 Galaxy and Lockheed C-141 StarLifter transport aircraft flying to Saudi Arabia. The SEALs who landed at Dhahran Air Base were the first Coalition special forces personnel to arrive in Saudi, and faced immediate problems. Not least of these problems was the fact that they had no base. Eventually a site called Half Moon Bay on the Saudi Arabian coast was chosen, and this site was then heavily fortified. Training began immediately, and this also involved close liaison with the Saudis' own SEAL units (though because the Saudi monarchy fears a coup mounted by special forces, and thus keeps the size of such units small, the Saudi SEALs comprised only two platoons).

The American SEALs immediately established a Naval Special Warfare Task Group at Ras al Ghar, Ras al Mishab and aboard a Kuwaiti barge

Above: US Navy SEALs were given the task of
fooling the Iraqis into believing that an
amphibious assault would be made on the
Kuwaiti coastline. This they did by mounting a
number of diversionary raids along the coast.

that had been captured by the Saudis. As with
other élite units in the Gulf, SEAL missions were
many and varied, and only a brief summary can
be given here. One of the first priorities was to

carry out covert beach reconnaissances along the Kuwaiti coastline in search of possible beach landing locations for a Marine Corps amphibious assault. SEALs also recaptured the Kuwaiti island of Qaruh, and mounted numerous diversionary raids against the Kuwaiti coast in an attempt, which was successful, to fool the Iraqis into believing that an amphibious assault was taking place, and thus force them to draw units away from the real frontline.

Force Recon Company deploys four-man teams for operations

The US Marines also had élite teams in the Gulf. These were the reconnaissance units. Force Recon Company, like the British SAS, deploys four-man teams for its operations. These can include long-range reconnaissance, target acquisition for artillery and naval gunfire, and beach reconnaissance. The similarities with the SAS do not end there. Each man is trained in one or more team specialities, such as weapons, medicine, demolition and signals. As mentioned above, the 'Recons' and the Green Berets had the border under tight control.

Another special forces unit that was deployed to the Gulf was the British Special Boat Service (SBS). Tasked with undertaking reconnaissance missions both in and out of the water, as well destroying enemy shipping in harbours, SBS soldiers are highly trained and effective. Prospective recruits to the SBS have to undergo intensive selection and training courses, which are equivalent in difficulty to those operated by the SAS. Volunteers for the SBS are drawn from the Royal Marines and must first pass a five-day

'acquaint' course in order to gain a place on the selection course proper. Since January 1994 this has been incorporated into a general 'special forces' selection with the SAS at their Stirling Lines headquarters in Hereford, in which volunteers for the SAS and SBS participate. The stringency of the SBS selection is as legendary as that of the SAS. Only five in every 50 volunteers pass the SBS course on average. If successful, the SBS candidate qualifies as a swimmer canoeist and is based at Poole in Dorset.

There is always close cooperation between the SAS and its maritime counterpart, which include squadron exchanges. If anything, the SBS is more clandestine than the SAS, but this has resulted in a partial limitation, as an SAS soldier from B Squadron explains:

'The Regiment has enjoyed massive publicity since the Iranian Embassy siege in 1980. The SBS has always fought hard to remain in the shadows, away from the limelight, but I think they regret that now. They are now under Army control and have not grown in size as we have.'

The SAS conducted cross-training with the SEALs and Green Berets

The Gulf War was the first time the two organisations had worked together since the Falklands conflict eight years before, when tragically an SBS man – Sergeant 'Kiwi' Hunt – had been killed accidentally during a 'blue-on-blue' fire-fight with an SAS patrol.

As usual, the friendly rivalry between the two units surfaced in the Gulf. The different terms of slang peculiar to each formation was a constant source of amusement:

'To us [the SAS] they were "Royal" or "Cabbage Head", and to them we were "Perc". Their slang is something we will never master. For example, when they talk about a night on the town they refer to "going ashore", whereas we say "let's get bladdered". They call the toilet the "heads" while we call it the "bog", and when they have a cup of tea it's called a "wet", while to us it's a "brew". No wonder they have a problem getting on in life – no fucker can understand them! It's worse when they have a meal. For example, after a late briefing the instructor told us to get our arses across to the cookhouse, get some scoff and then make our

PLAN OF CAMPAIGN

way back for the second half of the briefing. A good SB friend of mine complained: "Fucking scoff, it's scran and we eat in the galley not the fucking cookhouse" Unbelievable!'

As well as working with the SBS, the SAS conducted cross-training with the SEALs and Green Berets. The SEALs were endearingly known in the Regiment as 'hermans' on account of their size (after one of the characters in the TV series *The Munsters*). To the British they were 'bigger than a fucking big thing', and it was widely believed they could take on the Iraqi Republican Guard on their own. Their size caused much amusement, and generally brightened up what was a boring waiting period.

Cross-training with the Americans also brought another advantage: the SAS soldiers could 'liberate' their kit. There is a philosophy in the Regiment that if something looks nice and new and shiny it must be worth having. This stems partially from the sub-standard equipment that was the norm throughout the British Army up to the early 1980s:

'There was a lot of good kit floating about which the Yanks had brought in with them. Compared to us they were living like lords, and so at every opportunity we "liberated" kit and stores to make our life more bearable. About 10 years ago much of the kit used by the British Army was dross. Today, it must be said, most of it is first-class. For example, Gore-tex and the new chest webbing really is the "bizz". But old habits die hard, and whatever the Regiment receives we are always on the look out for something better.'

The Regiment was used to fighting in the desert, but a whole new scenario was the Iraqi threat to use chemical weapons. During the war with Iran, Saddam Hussein had been developing

nuclear and chemical warfare capabilities. This so alarmed the Israelis that they had bombed and destroyed Iraq's Osiraq primary nuclear facility near Baghdad in June 1981, thus lessening this particular danger. However, Iraq's chemical weapons programme had continued apace, and by the time of the Gulf War Saddam had a large chemical arsenal. What was worse was that he was prepared to use it. Evidence for this willingness is not hard to find: he had used chemical weapons against the Iranians in 1984, 1985 and 1986 during the Iran-Iraq War, as well as against his rebellious Kurdish subjects.

'As the choppers lifted off we started to tab to a rendezvous five kilometres away'

As the Coalition forces gathered in Saudi Arabia, the high command realised that there was a danger that the Iraqis might use chemical weapons against their forces. Therefore, Nuclear, Biological and Chemical (NBC) equipment and clothing were issued, and soldiers were inoculated against various biological diseases. No one really knew what the Iraqis would do (neither did Iraqi commanders on the ground, who knew that to use chemical weapons, which they were authorised to do from Baghdad, was to invite massive retaliation from the Allies, and certain death), and so everyone prepared for the worst. In the event chemical weapons were not used, though no one knew this in January 1991.

For the SAS this meant training in NBC suits. A member of A Squadron remembers one particular exercise:

'The threat of chemical warfare was constant, and during the training period with the Yanks we had carried out several scenarios in which we had come under gas attack. In the first couple of

days of January we were working with the Yanks, who had dropped us into the desert in a couple of Super Stallion helicopters. As the choppers lifted off we started to tab to a rendezvous five kilometres away, where a mobile patrol would come and pick us up. But halfway there we received the message that a "Scud" had just hit eight kilometres from where we were with a chemical warhead. It was only an exercise, but we had to tab the rest of the way in full NBC kit plus bergens. Believe me it was a very unpleasant experience, and one which we all dreaded. Nobody in the Regiment wanted to wage a war inside a "noddy" suit.'

AL-HUSSAIN Launcher

AL-ABBAS Launcher

CHAPTER 4

The Road Watch Patrols

As Saddam Hussein's air force and air defence network was dealt a fatal blow by Allied aircraft on the first day of the war, it seemed that little could affect the smooth running of the campaign. However, Saddam's forces in western Iraq then began firing Scud missiles at Israel. The Jewish state threatened to retaliate. If that happened the alliance would break apart. Therefore the Scuds had to be found and destroyed. The SAS was sent in to find them.

The anti-Scud SAS road watch patrols were a somewhat hasty answer to the problem of preventing Israel from entering the war. Saddam Hussein had pulled off a masterstroke in firing the Scuds at what he called the 'Zionist entity', and he temporarily wrested the initiative from the UN High Command in Riyadh.

In the few hours that remained before the Coalition air campaign started, Lieutenant-General Peter de la Billière and General Norman Schwarzkopf went over the SAS's missions in western Iraq. At this stage in the conflict the primary objective was still attacks on roads and communications centres, with general harassment as a secondary task. Well down the list at this time was the hunt for Scud surface-to-surface missile (SSM) launchers.

The 'balloon went up' during the night of 16/17 January 1991. While Coalition aircraft began their attacks on the enemy, Colonel Andrew Massey, the commanding officer of the Regiment at that time, began to move the whole of the SAS to its forward operating base (FOB) in western Saudi Arabia. Dozens of men, plus all their weapons, equipment and vehicles, were moved by RAF Hercules transport aircraft to the FOB, which was situated 900km (1448 miles) northwest of Riyadh.

Opposite: Iraqi Scud surface-to-surface missiles on display in Baghdad before the 1991 Gulf War.

At the start of the war the SAS was a very small cog in a very large machine: a unit that numbered around 250 men in a fighting force that totalled well over half a million men and women. It would have a job to do, but that job was relatively insignificant when compared to UN air and ground offensives that were planned, and the Coalition's overall aims in the war.

The overall objectives of the war, as dictated by Central Command (CENTCOM) in Riyadh, were as follows: to strike Iraq's political and military leadership, her command and control centres; to achieve and maintain air superiority in the skies over Kuwait and Iraq; to destroy Iraq's chemical, biological and nuclear capabilities; to destroy those Republican Guard units in the Kuwaiti theatre of operations (the politically reliable and militarily élite Republican Guard consisted of the *Hammurabi* and *Medina* Armoured Divisions, the *Tawakalna* Mechanised Division, three infantry divisions and a special forces division; though it spearheaded the invasion of Kuwait, the Republican Guard was in fact re-deployed in southeastern Iraq during the course of the war); and to liberate Kuwait. The first part of the operation consisted of an air campaign, the initial targets of which were enemy radar sites, electrical plants, communications towers and command posts. To achieve these objectives, the Coalition had assembled a colossal air fleet, consisting of over 2000 aircraft (a variety of modern fighters, bombers, attack and ground-attack aircraft, helicopters, reconnaissance and Airborne Warning And Control Systems [AWACS] models). To

Left: SAS vehicles near the Iraqi border in January 1991. All three road watch patrols were flown into enemy territory by RAF CH-47 Chinook helicopters – the vehicles were left behind.

counter this threat, the Iraqi air force could put into the skies around 750 fighters and ground-attack aircraft, plus a small number of aged Soviet bombers and transport aircraft. While these Iraqi air assets were not large or modern compared to those of the Coalition fleet, it was realised in Riyadh that Iraqi aircraft could inflict major damage on UN air assets and that they had therefore to be neutralised.

Thus, it was obvious that the first two days of the conflict held the key to air superiority. If the Iraqi air force could be dealt a crippling blow during this initial 48-hour period, it would never recover. The man responsible for planning the Coalition's air war, Lieutenant-General Charles Horner, commander of the US 9th Air Force, planned accordingly.

To win his part of the war, Horner had split the campaign into four phases

To win his part of the war, Horner had split the air campaign into four phases. Phase one would last an estimated 7-10 days, and would have three main objectives: to gain air superiority over Iraq and Kuwait; to destroy Iraq's strategic attack capability, her nuclear, chemical and biological production facilities, and her Scud missile launch and storage sites; and to disrupt Iraq's command and control structure. Phase two, expected to last three days, entailed the suppression of the air defences of those Iraqi forces deployed in and around Kuwait itself. Phase three, which would last from the end of the second phase until the beginning of the ground offensive, involved Allied aircraft attacking those targets in the first two phases, but with the emphasis on striking

Iraqi Army units in Kuwait. Phase four involved the provision of air support as and when required during the UN ground offensive. The Allied planners had certainly done their work well, but the first period would be critical.

The radar sites erupted into flames as the missiles found their targets

The first Coalition aircraft that would hit Iraq's comprehensive air-defence radar network were eight McDonnell Douglas AH-64 Apache attack helicopters from the crack US 101st Airborne Division, codenamed Task Force 'Normandy'. They took off just after dark on 16 January and headed towards two Iraqi air-defence radars to the west of Baghdad, approximately 700km (435 miles) inside enemy territory. The destruction of such facilities was vital if the Iraqis were to be blinded as to the whereabouts of Coalition aircraft in their air space. Arriving within 3-6km (1.8-3.7 miles) of their targets, the Apaches started their attack with salvoes of Hellfire missiles. The Hellfire is a missile that homes in on laser radiation reflected from the target, which is 'illuminated' by laser energy from the attacking aircraft or any other friendly designator. Armed with a 9kg (20lb) hollow-charge HE warhead, the Hellfire can penetrate the armour of all main battle tanks in service. The radar sites erupted into flames as the missiles found their targets. The Iraqi personnel manning these locations were killed either by the Hellfires or by the helicopters' 30mm cannon as the Apaches swooped in to finish the job. The sites had been totally destroyed. The Apaches hovered overhead for a few minutes to ensure nothing was left intact

(one of the reasons for using slow-moving helicopters for the mission was their ability to hover and carry out extensive damage assessment of the site), and then headed for friendly territory. The first aerial mission of the war had been a success.

At midnight on 16 January, Lockheed F-117 Night Hawk 'stealth' warplanes of the US Air Force's 415th Tactical Fighter Squadron took off from Khamis Mushait air base in the south of Saudi Arabia. They would be followed a short while later by more F-117s of the 416th Tactical Fighter Squadron, which took off from the same base. Already in the skies, meanwhile, Grumman E-2C Hawkeye and Boeing E-3B/C AWACS aircraft tracked and vectored Coalition aircraft onto their targets (the E-2 is a twin-turboprop carrier-borne AWACS aircraft, while the E-3 was developed from the airframe of the four-turbofan Boeing Model 707-320B airliner).

Unseen by Iraqi radar, the F-117s attacked 34 targets associated with the enemy's air-defence network. In addition, 52 BGM-109 Tomahawk cruise missiles launched from the battleships USS *Wisconsin* and *Missouri*, as well as the cruiser USS *San Jacinto*, hit enemy strategic targets (the Tomahawk proved itself to be one of the most potent weapons of the Gulf War. Carrying a 454kg (1000lb) high-explosive warhead and guided by an inertial navigation system updated by a terrain comparison and matching system, it acted as a precision-guided weapon for use at long ranges against fixed targets).

Their radar network seriously reduced in effectiveness, the Iraqis could do little to counter the

Right: Lieutenant-General Charles Horner, the man who planned the United Nations air campaign against Iraq. He made a major contribution to the eventual Allied victory.

second wave of Coalition fighters and attack
warplanes that hit them that night. McDonnell
Douglas F-15E Eagles and General Dynamics F-
111 all-weather attack aircraft of the US Air
Force decimated Scud missile launch sites, missile storage bunkers and airfields. As these attacks
were made, F-15E Eagles and US Navy Grumman F-14 Tomcats provided fighter support,
while Iraqi anti-aircraft defences were suppressed
by other F-14s, US Navy Vought A-7 Corsairs
and McDonnell Douglas F/A-18 Hornets carrying AGM-88 High-Speed Anti-Radiation Missiles (HARMs). In addition, British Panavia Tor-
nado long-range interdiction aircraft destroyed
enemy targets with Air-Launched Anti-Radiation Missiles (ALARMs). Those enemy radars
located at Iraqi anti-aircraft defence sites were
jammed by American aircraft such as the Grumman (General Dynamics) EF-111A Raven,
Grumman EA-6B Prowler and Lockheed EC-
130 'Compass Call' aircraft using jamming pods
to blind and confuse enemy systems.

One by one Iraqi targets were attacked and systematically destroyed

One by one Iraqi high-priority targets were
attacked and systematically destroyed. For example, 53 US Air Force F-111Fs attacked 12 sites,
including the airfields at Balad and Jalibah in Iraq
and Ali Salem and Ahmed al-Jaber in Kuwait
(where Scuds were believed to be hidden in the

*Right: An American AH-64 Apache attack
helicopter. A force of Apaches from the 101st
Airborne Division were the first aircraft to hit
Iraq's air-defence network on the night of 16
January. At the start of the air war the SAS was
very much on the sidelines.*

hardened aircraft shelters). The F-111s also struck chemical weapons storage bunkers at H3 airfield, Salman Pak and Ad Diwaniyah. For good measure, during the night of 17 January three F-111Fs, supported by two EF-111s, attacked Saddam Hussein's summer palace at Tikrit, turning it into a pile of rubble. Unfortunately, the dictator was not at home.

On the second day of the war, the Iraqis had fired one Scud missile at Dhahran

The air war had begun superbly. The statistics were almost too good to be true. The initial wave of air strikes consisted of 671 sorties. Despite the heavy flak that some of the Coalition aircraft had encountered, especially over Baghdad, there had been no losses. In addition, the Iraqi air force had hardly been seen. For example, up to midnight of 17 January the Allies had flown 2107 sorties compared to 24 combat missions undertaken by the Iraqis. All the planning and preparations seemed to be paying off. It seemed that the war could be conducted and won by conventional air and ground forces alone. Schwarzkopf's beliefs seemed vindicated: there seemed little need for special forces. Yet there was a dark cloud on the horizon.

On the second day of the war, 18 January, the Iraqis had fired one Scud missile at Dhahran, a major Saudi airport and military base. The threat to such high-value targets had been realised by the Coalition High Command, so 132 Raytheon

Left: A battery of Patriot surface-to-air missiles guards against Scud attacks in Saudi Arabia. The sudden demand for Patriot in Saudi and Israel caused stockpiles in America to run low.

MIM-104 Patriot surface-to-air missile (SAM) launchers had been positioned to protect Riyadh, Dhahran and other locations. The Patriot is an advanced SAM system, and, it was hoped, one able to counter the Scud threat. A Patriot system consists of a multi-role radar, an engagement control station and up to eight quadruple SAM launchers. The radar performs all the surveillance, acquisition, target tracking, identification friend or foe, and illumination functions for the missiles, while the engagement control station controls all radar scheduling, weapon allocation and target prioritisation. The missile launchers themselves are mounted on semi-trailers, and hold four flight-ready missiles. Fortuitously, in the light of events in the Gulf, the missiles were modified for anti-tactical ballistic missile capabilities. The target is illuminated by the Patriot's radar system, and then the target reflections are relayed to the engagement control station on the ground. The information is processed by the fire-control computer, which transmits guidance commands back to the missile via the data link.

Seven Scuds streaked into the sky and headed west towards Israel

The Patriot batteries protecting the large air base at Dhahran were from the 2nd Battalion of the 11th Air Defense Artillery Brigade. As one Iraqi Scud missile hurtled towards the air base at an estimated speed of 6400km/h (3975mph), a Patriot streaked from its launch canister and into the sky. The theory was simple enough: in the quarter of a millisecond in which the Patriot passed the Scud, the former would detonate, throwing out 300 ice-cubed sized cubes of metal

that would destroy the Iraqi weapon. A split-second miscalculation would mean some of the Scuds slipping through. That night the Scud did not slip through, and the Patriot legend was born. In fact, Patriot was far less effective than at first claimed. For example, the Israelis conducted studies of the Scuds that were engaged by Patriots over Israel. They found that only nine per cent of engagements resulted in confirmed warhead kills, though to be fair in other cases the Patriots did knock the Scuds off course. Needless to say, this information was kept secret until the war had ended.

While the Americans were congratulating themselves on the effectiveness of their Patriot system, in western Iraq several Iraqi Scud mobile launcher teams and their vehicle convoys were driving through the blackness of the desert. As scores of Coalition warplanes criss-crossed the skies above them, the men hastily prepared their missiles, their work made all the more speedy through fear of being attacked by Allied aircraft. However, none of the crews was spotted and they all managed to fire their missiles. Seven Scuds streaked into the sky and headed west towards Israel. Two struck Haifa, three landed on Tel Aviv and the rest fell in unpopulated areas. Although, miraculously, there were no serious casualties, Saddam had suddenly 'upped the stakes' in the Gulf conflict.

Although the missiles that hit Israel were armed with conventional warheads, the Israelis feared that subsequent ones would not be. Saddam had made frequent threats against the Jewish state. On one occasion, for example, when denying that Iraq had nuclear weapons, he stated: 'Why should we need an atomic bomb? Don't they know that we have the binary chem-

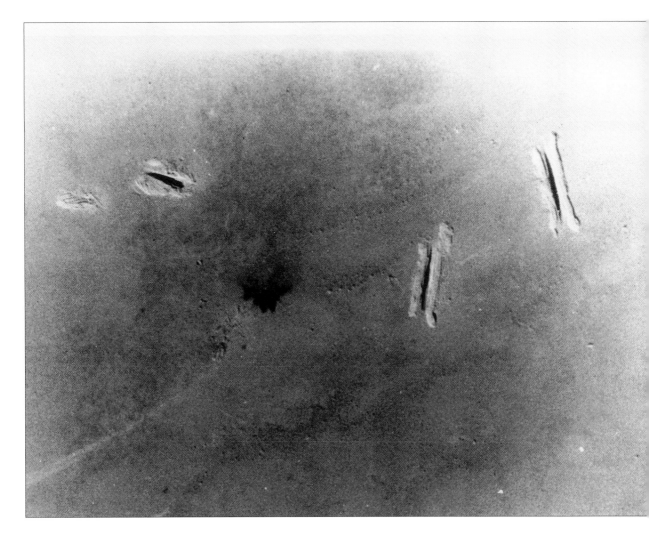

ical weapons to cause fire to devour half of the Zionist entity if the Zionist entity, which has atomic bombs, dared attack Iraq?' (A note on binary weapons: early chemical weapons had a warhead containing only one chemical agent, and the warhead was thus known as a unitary warhead. However, the contents of these unitary warheads were often corrosive, and this caused the containers to 'weep'. With a binary warhead

Above: US Air Force photographs of Iraqi Scud launch sites in western Iraq. Note the Scud trenches, missile firing blast marks, vehicle marks around the blast and the small berm for the protection of the ground crew.

two agents are held separately, and thus harmlessly: only when they have been dropped or fired are they mixed to produce a lethal chemical agent). In May 1990 Saddam had declared: 'If

Above: The remains of a Scud fired at Saudi Arabia, which landed in an American base. The decision by Saddam Hussein to launch the missiles at Israel nearly split the UN Coalition.

it [Israel] uses weapons of mass destruction against our nation, we will use against it the weapons of mass destruction in our possession.' To the Israelis it seemed that Iraq was about to rain a chemical and biological storm down upon them, or, even worse, a nuclear holocaust.

One thing was certain: the Israelis would not stand by and let this happen. However, if they were to launch attacks upon Iraq, it might split the Coalition. In particular, it would have been very doubtful that the Arab members, especially Egypt and Syria, would allow themselves to become indirect allies of Israel. Saddam had played a masterful stroke, but Schwarzkopf and de la Billière, with the help of the American administration in Washington, were to better it.

The Israelis were naturally outraged by the missile attacks. They would clearly not procrastinate while chemical and biological weapons landed among them – the spectre of Jews being gassed for the second time in half a century loomed large. The Americans in particular recognised the dangers to the Coalition, and made frantic efforts to pacify the Israelis. Secretary of State James Baker telephoned the Israeli Prime Minister, Yitzhak Shamir, and tried to reassure him: 'We are going after western Iraq full bore. There is nothing that your air force can do that we are not already doing. If there is, tell us, and we will do it. We appreciate your restraint, and please don't play into Saddam's hands.' Shamir was persuaded, and went back to the Israeli cabinet to relay the news that the Allies were doing their utmost.

However, not all in the Israeli administration were convinced. In particular, Moshe Arens, the defence minister, was sceptical. He had, in any case, his own plans for dealing with the Scuds. He had ordered Israeli troops to practise in the Negev Desert for just such a scenario. Heliborne troops, escorted by Israeli air force aircraft, would attack the Scud batteries in western Iraq. For weeks these troops had been rehearsing against mock Scud batteries. The operation would entail flying through Saudi or Jordanian air space. The Israelis knew that neither would sanction such a move. This was of little consequence, however, for if it came to it the Israelis could destroy the Jordanian air force in a matter of minutes. The only problem was that this

would undoubtedly plunge the whole of the Middle East into war. This did not figure high in Arens' equation, though, for the only thing that interested him was striking back at Iraq (he also believed that forbearance had eroded 40 years of deterrence based on the concept of instant retaliation). Baker pleaded with Arens: 'I hope that you won't respond or retaliate. Please consider this a formal request for moderation.'

While the Israelis thought about moderation, more Scuds fell on their country. On 19 January, for example, two of them hit Tel Aviv, injuring 17 people, while another two fell harmlessly into unpopulated areas. Though the casualty rate appeared light, recent research has confirmed that many Israelis died as a result of the fear and anxiety the Scud attacks caused. The exact number of people who died in this way will never be accurately known. And at the time a lot of people believed that the next Scud might contain chemical or biological agents.

Israeli action seemed increasingly likely as January drew to a close

The Americans had offered Patriot missile batteries as a defence against the Scuds. At first Arens refused them; now he welcomed them and asked that they be despatched to Israel as quickly as possible. The first arrived on 20 January. The crew of the battery worked with haste to get it into position and working. Unbeknown to them, it would be another two days before more Iraqi Scuds hit Israel.

Meanwhile, over western Iraq, F-15E Strike Eagles had been designated to hunt for the Scuds and their mobile launchers. These aircraft of the

Above: Patriot missiles streak into the sky to engage Scuds over Tel Aviv. The Iraqis wanted to provoke Israel into joining the war, thus causing Syria and Egypt to leave the UN Coalition.

US 4th Tactical Fighter Wing hunted day and night for their prey, but with limited success. The Eagle is a magnificent warplane, and has an all-weather ground-attack capability. Two aspects of the aircraft's equipment would, it was hoped, be able to locate and destroy the mobile Scud launchers. The first was the Low Altitude Navigation and Targeting Infra-Red for Night (LANTIRN) night vision and target-acquisition system. This consists of two pods, a navigation pod containing a wide field-of-view forward-looking infra-red (FLIR) sensor and a terrain-following radar, and a targeting pod containing a narrow field-of-vision FLIR and a laser designator. Data from the navigation FLIR and terrain-following radar are displayed as images on the warplane's head-up display (HUD), which gives the pilot a visual representation of the terrain ahead, together with steering instructions and a mass of tactical information. In this way the warplane can fly at low level at night and in poor weather. The targeting pod has an automatic target recognition device that scans the field of view for preset target types, such as tanks. When an appropriate target is located, the device automatically locks onto it and passes the information to air-to-surface missiles with imaging infra-red guidance. The missiles can be launched either manually or automatically, and the system is so quick that multiple missile launches are possible on a single pass. In addition, the targeting pod's laser designator can be used to illuminate targets for laser-guided bombs.

The laser-guided bomb, specifically the GBU-10 'Paveway' weapons carried by the Eagles in western Iraq, was the second item of equipment in the anti-Scud search. A laser-guided bomb operates by using its semi-active laser homing device to home in on radiation reflected off a target that is illuminated by a laser designator. The bomb's seeker head contains a silicon detector array divided into quadrants, and the laser radiation that is received by the detectors is converted into electrical impulses that the guidance computer uses to convert into steering commands for the canard control surfaces. The target can be illuminated by a laser designator on the attacking aircraft itself, on a second aircraft, or by a laser designator on the ground.

This, then, was the theory, but the reality was very different. The 'great Scud hunt' was reaping little or no rewards for the Eagles, and the frustration started to grow. The Iraqis became very adept at hiding and masking their Scud launchers. They used civilian trucks as mobile launchers, storing them underground during the day and then using them at night. This should not have mattered to the Eagles, but they were also being fooled by the great number of decoys the Iraqis were using. Something that looked like a mobile Scud launcher and was emitting a heat signature might in fact just be a decoy with a paraffin lamp burning beside it. The grim truth was that Coalition aircraft never found a vehicle that could be positively identified as a mobile Scud launcher.

Israeli action seemed increasingly likely as January drew to a close and as more Scuds hit her cities: one on Tel Aviv on 22 January, causing three deaths, one the next day that fell on an unpopulated area, and eight on 25 January, all aimed at Tel Aviv but all destroyed by Patriots, though debris from the missiles did kill two and injured a further 69.

The SAS was now ordered to search out the Scuds in western Iraq. The Regiment, in the space of a few days, had gone from having a fairly minor part in the war to having the responsibility of keeping the Coalition together. It approached its task in its usual stoical manner. The days before they were sent into Iraq had been frustrating for the men of the Regiment:

'The war was under way. The sky above us buzzed with aircraft heading towards the border. As we finished our early morning fizz [physical fitness], the sun was just starting to toast the ground. We hadn't been able to do much in the last couple of days, but we knew we wouldn't be here for ever. The base was very busy: American A-10s, helicopters and a couple of British Hercs were packed on the tarmac.'

The men were itching to get at the enemy, and in their more idle moments wondered what was becoming of their adversaries, as a member of B Squadron relates:

'As we were waiting to go for scoff, a mate of mine from another squadron appeared and we exchanged ditts. "I wonder what those fuckin' ragheads are doing right now," my mate said, looking towards the border. "Probably picking their noses in the bottom of a trench," I replied.'

As the orders went out from Riyadh, the men were assembled and briefed. This was in addition

Below: Israeli citizens don gas masks during a Scud attack scare. In western Iraq, meanwhile, Allied aircraft and the SAS desperately searched for the missiles and their launchers.

SAS GULF WARRIORS

Above: The McDonnell Douglas F-15E Strike Eagle, one of the most advanced strike aircraft in the world. Though these aircraft were committed to the great Scud hunt, the results were disappointing. The American and British special forces teams on the ground, on the other hand, achieved much better results.

to their routine daily brief, and was 'welcomed by everyone'. The SAS would tackle the Scud threat in three ways. First, static road watch patrols would be mounted to report the movement of Scud traffic, and then direct F-15s onto the convoys. Second, fighting columns would roam western Iraq to hunt for the missile launchers. Third, SAS parties would cut Iraq's concealed communications links to prevent orders being sent to the launch teams.

The road watch patrols would be made up of three patrols of eight men each, and would monitor the three Main Supply Routes (MSRs) that went from the Euphrates valley to the Jordanian hills in the west. The men were to be drawn from B Squadron. After the teams had been assembled, a major from the Intelligence Corps gave them a briefing concerning mobile Scuds and the morale of the enemy troops. Then the men were issued with a warning order, a military term indicating they should be prepared to move at a moment's notice. After weeks of uncertainty and unhurried activity, B Squadron was suddenly plunged into a fevered state. The men checked their equipment to make sure they were ready to 'rock and roll'. This included the main patrol radios, tactical beacons (TACBEs), plus the usual bergen checklist: water purification tablets, demolition charges, Nuclear, Biological, Chemical (NBC) suits, Polaroid camera (for photographs that could be used for intelligence evaluations), night vision scope and glucose tablets for energy. The TACBE was an old piece of kit and caused the Regiment serious problems in Iraq. They were originally designed for use in Europe against the Russians by transmitting short encoded bursts of information on a high frequency, but in the desert interference from the ionosphere crippled their capability. After the war the Ministry of Defence procured new radios for the Regiment, after it carried out a major review of available 'emergency comms systems', including the satellite units used by the US Special Forces during the war. Each patrol

carried other essential equipment. Near the top of the list was the collapsible plastic water carrier, grandly called the 'piss pot'. A member of 'B' Squadron explains:

'The Iraqis may have had mobile Scuds, but the Regiment has had mobile piss pots for years. It is easy to just piss anywhere in the desert, but as we all know it stinks and will soon attract interest from ants, making life very uncomfortable when you are in a static position. It can also attract animals, which can compromise your position. The plastic container opens up to carry a few pints, and once in the field is camouflaged with some hessian to avoid any shine from the sun hitting the plastic. On the move the container is emptied as soon as possible.' In addition, all excrement is bagged and then disposed of later, as anything that smells has the potential to compromise the operation.

Each man has those items that are regarded as being essential to him

Aside from the patrol essentials, each man has those items that are regarded as being essential to his personal well-being. These can be quite eccentric. This from another member of the same squadron:

'Everyone has their own favourites, but a lifesaver for me has always been a tube of Vaseline, especially if we had to tab great distances and suffered from foot injuries. This all goes back to when I first joined the Regiment. After a year-long build-up of weekend training to prepare for Selection, my feet were shagged. At the beginning of a training plod we were told to take off our boots and select a pair from a bag that had been dumped on the ground. I quickly grabbed what I thought was the right size. However, the laces were a bit short, and by the time I had finished the 10km (16-mile) phase of the test my feet were in bits. One of the instructors told me about covering my feet in Vaseline before a long tab. It works wonders, and the advice has stayed with me since my early days with the Regiment.'

The soldiers of the SAS are given quite a lot of leeway when it comes to personal equipment, and this was reflected in the way each man 'tooled up' before the road watch patrols. Some had chest rigs that incorporated a belt order, while others wore a standard '58-pattern yoke which supported a massive belt order of pouches carrying water, ammunition, survival kit, emergency food, TACBE and a Global Positioning System (GPS) navigation aid.

'The thud, thud, thud of the rotors got louder as the pilot pulled power'

The patrol medics carried equipment pertinent to their duties: 'I had spent several weeks on an intensive course arranged by the Ministry of Defence with the National Health Service. I worked with paramedics in several cities across the country to gain first-hand experience of dealing with serious injuries and trauma.' All the medicines carried by the medic are clearly marked. In this way if he is killed the others will know what to use his supplies for. Thus containers holding tablets for diarrhoea and pain killing are marked 'anti-shits' and 'pain' respectively.

As the time for the men to deploy neared, each patrol received its Orders Group (O Group) briefing. During this they received the facts and

figures for the job, after which they would be deployed. This is SAS standard operating procedure (SOP), and ensures that no one has the chance to talk about the mission before they go. In the majority of cases this means that once a team has been briefed, it is simply a matter of them waiting for the aircraft and vehicles. 'Either way you are in operational isolation from other SAS squadron members – you have information they don't.'

The three road watches were to be inserted by Chinook helicopter. The thoroughness of the SAS was matched by that of the RAF helicopter crews, who had spent a considerable time at the briefings going through procedures in the event of something going wrong on the ground. If it did, the helicopter crews advised the SAS teams to stay with the aircraft – the percentage chances of getting out alive were apparently greater. However, SAS soldiers like to be in control of their own destiny:

'As I recalled from my Para [Parachute Regiment] days, there was nothing quite like the feeling of vulnerability when you are sat inside an aircraft with someone else in charge of your life.' The briefings complete, the three road watch patrols headed for their drop-off points: 'Lifting out of the airstrip was just like getting airborne in a Chinook anywhere in the UK. The thud, thud, thud of the rotors got louder as the pilot pulled power to lift the bird, then nose-down we swept along the runway and into the night sky. Both pilots were wearing night vision goggles, and almost immediately we started our low-level flight path.'

Everyone tried to get some sleep, though it was difficult with the deafening noise in the fuselage. Within what seemed to be no time at all,

the loadmaster was waving his illuminated wand to get the occupants' attention – five minutes to the refuel stop. The fuel stop consisted of a unit containing British and American personnel at the Iraqi-Saudi border. The SAS soldiers were very impressed by what they saw: 'It was a highly professional team, everything was under camouflage.' Inside the Chinooks were massive inflatable rubber tanks that contained a large fuel reserve. 'As we sat on the ground a Crab climbed

Above: A Chinook helicopter warms up its engines before another mission. British Chinooks in the Gulf were fitted with internal long-range fuel tanks, which limited space inside the fuselage for SAS teams.

aboard wearing shemagh and goggles. Inside the fuselage he took off his headdress and pulled a huge flask out of his jacket and gave us all a quick brew – what a star! Another member of the ground crew appeared at the back of the aircraft

Above: SAS and Bedouin on friendly terms in Oman in the 1970s. In the Gulf War the Regiment was warned to keep clear of these nomads, as they were offered rewards by the Iraqis for the surrender of captured UN military personnel.

and waved a sign announcing that this was the "last stop for fuel in Saudi".'

The Chinooks took off and headed into enemy territory. When they reached their drop-off points, the aircraft disgorged their occupants.

The commander of the South Road Watch team decided to abandon his mission almost immediately. The ground he and his men would have to operate in was a gravel plain. There was no cover and they would have been quickly compromised. The men left in the Chinook they arrived in. The story of the North Road Watch is told in the next chapter. What about the Central Road Watch team? The following account was told to the author by one of those who took part.

'We were all ready and knew that as soon as we hit the deck we would be out and away from the landing site. Fresh, cold air hit our faces as we jumped off the ramp seconds before the aircraft touched down and threw ourselves on the ground as a protection against an ambush. This is a procedure known as an immediate action, and is second nature to the men in the Regiment. Our heavy bergens were quickly unloaded, and a check was made to make sure we had not left anything behind.

'From bitter experience I knew it was better to waste a couple of extra seconds checking nothing was left than to wait until the aircraft was airborne and realise that something had been forgotten. When I was with the Paras I remember being dropped off in South Armagh and scrambling out of the Wessex as quickly and as professionally as I could. We were out so fast I hadn't noticed that the barrel of my light machine gun (LMG) had been left behind. The LMGs used in Ulster had been modified to take 7.62mm ammunition, and it was easy for the barrel to come off by simply banging the release button on the left-hand side of the weapon. When the Wessex circled and landed back in front of us, one of the crewmen stood in the doorway and waved my barrel at us – I was about as popular as a dose in a convent. You can't afford such fuck-ups when you're deep in enemy territory.

'The cab [helicopter] lifted off, a crewman raising his thumbs to wish us good luck – we were on our own. Quickly we mounted up and, after orientating ourselves, moved out towards the area where we could monitor the MSR. After a two-hour tab we were desperately trying to find a lying-up place, but all we could see was flat, horrible ground with no cover. As the sun came up we opted to make the best of what we had. One team would work the day with another in a defensive position 100 metres (328ft) behind the front team. We made small scrapes among the rocks, but it was more or less open countryside and our camouflage and concealment skills would be seriously tested.

'Most people think that the desert is empty – forget it! Every man and his dog seemed to be on the road. It was alive with traffic, with civilians pouring west and military traffic heading towards Kuwait. We identified the vehicle types and the possible stores they were carrying, which would help the intelligence boys. Every serviceable truck appeared to have been pressed into service, many of them towing small field guns.

'We were all shitting it with regard to Saddam's biological and chemical weapons'

'However, there was no sign of the mobile Scud platforms or Iraqi troops dressed in NBC kit. We were all shitting it with regard to Saddam's biological and chemical weapons. We sat wearing our Noddy suits and in the sun we baked. I felt like a fucking "boil in the bag" chicken. I just hoped that I would not have to use the compo pens in the top of my respirator bag or fight in a chemical environment.

'Our volume of kit was incredible. In fact, we had more kit than a fucking big kit thing, but it was all needed. At night those of us who had them donned padded jackets and gloves, while others pulled on Norwegian Army jumpers. Everyone put on their woolly hats. When off stag, sleep was grabbed among the rocks, webbing still worn and weapons at the ready.

'We were ordered to remain on the ground for four days, but the potential for compromise was too great, and so late in the afternoon the boss took the decision to abandon the watch and bug out before we were bounced. The game plan was to tab to a rendezvous 7km [4.35 miles] away, where we could be lifted out by helicopter at 0400 hours the following morning. In Ulster we used a small strobe light to direct helicopters into a direct landing, but in Iraq the flash would be seen for miles around, so a signal on a red torch was used instead.

'After less than an hour's plod we all went to ground, the front man had heard activity up ahead. Two men went forward with night vision scopes to discover the noise was coming from Iraqi soldiers, whose column of vehicles was parked alongside the MSR. We could have ignored them and continued with our journey, but there was a danger that they might ambush the helicopter. Besides, there was a chance to recover a couple of prisoners, which we could take back to Saudi Arabia with us.

'We sprinted forward and were on top of them before they knew what hit them'

'As there was plenty of air power available, we called in an air strike. It took almost 35 minutes to materialise, though, and when it did the aircraft moved straight in on the target. Our aim was to monitor the attack and watch to see if any Iraqis legged it. The first aircraft screamed away above our heads. We heard a thump, followed by a large fireball that engulfed one of the vehicles. Four more explosions followed, crippling the convoy. The SBS had bagged the first oper-ational special job in the Gulf, and another SAS team had bagged the first contact, so we wanted to be the first to grab a prisoner. Any raghead who attempted to leg it from the scene would, we hoped, run right past us. Behind the convoy a huge sand bank made a quick escape impossible – the obvious route was across the road towards us.

'Six of them came towards us, but then suddenly disappeared from sight. They had taken cover themselves and were waiting for the attack to finish. We couldn't afford to wait around as Iraqi support could arrive at any minute. So we had to go and get them. We sprinted forward and were on top of them before they knew what hit them. We were firing our weapons and finding our targets. Seconds later it was all over. Four of them lay dead and two had minor upper-body injuries. As far as we were concerned they were "walking wounded". A search revealed papers and identity cards, the usual stuff. We patched up their wounded and then moved them out. I don't think they had ever moved so fast or over such a distance. The two of them were very quickly out of breath.

'Three hours later we reached our RV [rendezvous] and rested the prisoners, giving them food as we waited to be picked up. One of them was an officer, and we were quietly pleased that the job had not been wasted.'

The team was picked up by Chinook and flown back to base, everyone relieved that they had made it back alive.

Thus ended the road watch patrols, an audacious plan but one which ultimately failed. All special forces operations are high risk, and some have to be aborted. That they failed was no reflection on the men concerned or their equip-

Above: SAS soldiers pose beside their heavily armed Land Rover behind the lines in Iraq. The road watch patrols had been flown in by helicopter, the use of vehicles being ruled because of the urgency of the situation.

ment. They simply could not perform their task in the terrain they were inserted into. Better to live to fight another day. In any case, only one of the Regiment's strategies for finding the Scuds had failed. Another, the mobile fighting columns, were on their way. They would be much more successful in searching out the elusive foe. The lessons learned from the road watch patrols could be digested – future operations would benefit from their experience. There it should have ended. But the experiences of the North Road Watch team, codenamed 'Bravo Two Zero', ensured that this particular part of the SAS's campaign in the 1991 Gulf War will always be remembered.

CHAPTER 5

Race to the Border

The exploits of the SAS North Road Watch patrol, codenamed 'Bravo Two Zero', have become known around the world. The story is one of heroism, self-sacrifice and sheer determination set against the background of poor intelligence, hasty decisions in Riyadh and inadequate logistical support, and is also the story of probably the greatest single feat of endurance performed by an SAS soldier in the history of the Regiment.

It is not the intention here to paraphrase or summarise in detail the book written by Sergeant Andy McNab, the commander of the North Road Watch patrol, that describes the exploits of his SAS team, nor the book written by another team member, Corporal Chris Ryan, entitled *The One That Got Away*, which describes his thrilling escape to the Syrian border; rather, this chapter will examine the tactical decisions taken by McNab and his men, as well as the choices they made regarding personal equipment and SAS methods of insertion.

The story of the team, codenamed 'Bravo Two Zero', is now, thanks to the best-selling book of the same name, probably one of the best-known SAS operations ever. It is the enthralling story of eight SAS soldiers, landed 300km (185 miles) behind enemy lines, who were compromised when an enemy force set up camp almost on top of them. They made frantic and heroic efforts to escape, but only one did so, Corporal Chris Ryan, to Syria. Of the other seven men, three died and four were captured. McNab was one of those captured, and half his book is devoted to his experiences at the hands of the Iraqis. Needless to say, it makes for grim reading. Mentally and physically abused, he was lucky to live to tell his tale. When he was even-

Opposite: Sergeant Andy McNab, the commander of 'Bravo Two Zero', photo-graphed with the equipment load he took with him into Iraqi territory.

Above: 'Bravo Two Zero' on the tailgate of the Chinook just prior to their departure. Chris Ryan is on the extreme left (face covered). Those with faces uncovered are, from left to right, Bob Consiglio, 'Legs' Lane and Vince Phillips.

tually released he had a medical check. He was found to have a dislocated shoulder, ruptured muscles in his back, scar tissues on his kidneys, burns on his thighs and the loss of dexterity in his hands. Worse, he was also diagnosed as having hepatitis, no doubt a result of being forced to eat his own excrement. The treatment of McNab and other captured British and American servicemen by the Iraqis during the war was abso-

lutely appalling, and it is to the eternal shame of the United Nations (UN) in general that no war crimes charges were brought against the Iraqis who administered this treatment.

The story of 'Bravo Two Zero' is one of heroism, stoicism and courage in the face of adversity. That said, it should not blind people to the fact that the mission was a complete failure. It failed not because the men were ill-trained or unprepared, but because they were inserted into an area that was crawling with enemy forces, in addition to a hostile population that had been told to be on the lookout for 'infidel' soldiers and airmen.

Success with regard to special forces operations is all about intelligence. Timely, accurate information is essential to the successful planning and execution of élite missions. History is littered with operations that have failed because of poor intelligence. For example, during the Vietnam War US aerial photographic intelligence in the autumn of 1970 revealed that there were 55 American POWs being held at a prison compound at Son Tay, 37km (23 miles) west of Hanoi. The US Special Forces, the Green Berets, were ordered to plan and carry out the rescue of these POWs. The planning and preparation for the raid was extensive. It was estimated that the best time for the mission would be between 20 and 25 October, when the weather would be most favourable. A mock-up of the prison was constructed at Eglin Air Force Base in Florida, and it was dismantled during the day and set up again at night to prevent it being spotted by Soviet spy satellites (the information would then have been passed on to the North Vietnamese). The strike force consisted of three groups, and detailed rehearsals were carried out to ensure every man knew what his task would be during the actual mission. The assault itself was practised many times, and alternative plans were formulated in case one of the three teams failed to make it to the target.

The raid commenced during the evening of 20 November 1970 and was flawlessly executed, aside from one thing: there were no prisoners at the site. This fact had not been picked up by intelligence because far too much reliance had been placed upon photographic sources, and no one had bothered to put any agents on the ground to verify the photographs. The raid was a complete failure.

It was not quite the same for the men of 'Bravo Two Zero'. In McNab's book it is stated that the team later learnt that there were two Iraqi armoured divisions between the border and the team's first position. This is not quite true. The Regiment does all it can to ensure the success of missions. It had sent reconnaissance teams into the area, and they had reported the presence of Iraqi forces. Nevertheless, Riyadh, and specifically the Americans, insisted that the SAS be sent in. It was a small price to pay, it would seem, to keep Israel out of the war. The same view was not held by the commander of B Squadron, who got into a series of furious arguments over sending his men into an enemy-infested area. However, he was overruled and the mission went ahead. There was also another major problem, which does not seem to have been impressed upon the patrol members at all, and that was the fact that the local population were very keen-eyed, even more so than enemy soldiers.

SAS teams spent weeks and months living among the native people

Soldiers and civilians living in the West, who come from mostly urban, socially mobile environments, often misunderstand the mentality of Third World rural peoples. The latter tend to live in closed, tight-knit communities where outsiders are viewed with suspicion, even hostility. It is a lesson that was learned by the SAS in Malaya during the 1950s, Borneo during the 1960s and Oman during the 1970s. In those instances SAS teams spent weeks and months living near or among the native people. Slowly, the soldiers gained the trust of the local population, although it was a very painstaking and fraught process. Cultural and religious practices had to be respected, and individual troopers had to learn the indigenous tongues. These procedures now form part of the Regiment's 'hearts and minds' procedures (patrol medics often have to learn midwifery and veterinary skills to treat the wives and animals of the local men). In Iraq this was not possible for two reasons. First, the campaign was not one of counter-insurgency. The SAS was part of a UN force waging conflict against Iraq, so it was not there to subvert the Iraqi populace against Saddam Hussein (contrary to popular opinion, the UN did not have a remit to change the regime in Iraq). Second, the Iraqi population was hostile towards soldiers, sailors and airmen of the coalition, especially its Western members (the governments of the Allies, and their representatives at the UN, liked to maintain the facade that the war was solely against Saddam Hussein and his henchmen; inhabitants of towns and cities who were bombed daily, and had their sewage, water and electricity facilities knocked out, thought differently).

This being the case, remaining hidden from prying eyes can be extremely difficult. Locals are

Below: Two RAF Tornados fly low over the desert during a sortie into Iraq in late January 1991. Allied air superiority meant 'Bravo Two Zero' did not have to worry about Iraqi aircraft.

very 'switched on' when it comes to their immediate environment. In Iraq, the discovery of strangers would result in wild shouts and hollering, and the certainty of the authorities being alerted. This is what happened to 'Bravo Two Zero': the members of this team were discovered by a small boy tending a herd of goats. In addition, the nomadic Bedouins who roamed the region were on the lookout for Western servicemen – partly, no doubt, to claim the rewards that were being offered.

If the planners in Riyadh had known of the concentration of enemy forces in the area, so the official line goes, the road watch patrols would not have been sent in. General Norman Sch-

Above: A US Navy F-14 Tomcat, one of the many Allied aircraft that conducted the air campaign against Iraq. The intensity of Allied air operations prevented 'Bravo Two Zero' from being inserted on the night of 19 January.

warzkopf himself admitted as much to McNab after the latter's release from captivity. But by then the damage had been done and three of his team were dead. However, as stated above, Riyadh did know, and still the SAS was sent in (the role of sacrificial lamb is not one the Regiment likes to assume!).

McNab's team was given two tasks: to locate and destroy the Iraqi communications landlines in the northern Main Supply Route (MSR), and

locate and destroy Scud mobile missile launchers. They were told that the landlines were the way that Saddam was getting orders to the mobile launch teams – all other communications methods had been destroyed. Allied aircraft had done an effective job in destroying the pylons and transmitters above ground, which was ironic since it had been the Americans who had helped build them in the first place. In 1985, for example, during the Iran-Iraq War, US military specialists advised Iraq on establishing 'electronic walls' along the Iraqi-Iranian border. Later that year the Americans concluded a cooperation agreement with Iraq, part of which concerned help with communications. If the landlines could be destroyed, so went the theory, then the Iraqi leadership would have no way of contacting its Scud launcher units. Without direct orders from Saddam himself, the commanders on the ground would not fire the missiles (initiative among junior commanders was not a feature of the Iraqi armed forces, especially since any unauthorised decision making was likely to result in the perpetrator being executed for treason).

B Squadron's logistical backup left a lot to be desired at that time. The conditions at the SAS forward operating base (FOB) were appalling. McNab's team were forced to sleep on the ground round their Land Rover vehicles because there was no shelter available (the squadron sergeant-major had been instructed to ship the squadron tents to Saudi Arabia, but had decided against it because he thought the weather would

Left: SAS and locals in Oman in the 1970s. Many SAS operations in Third World countries have involved 'hearts and minds' programmes. In Iraq however, as 'Bravo Two Zero' found to its costs, the locals were invariably hostile.

be very warm and they wouldn't be needed!). Therefore, the men were forced to use the camouflage netting on the Land Rover vehicles for cover. In addition, there weren't any tables or chairs to be had anywhere, and so the men were forced to take their meals sitting on the floor. For supposedly one of the world's premier élite units it was a sorry state of affairs.

Anyone is free to criticise the plan of action, regardless of rank or experience

The decision where to insert the team was left to McNab and his men. This was the subject of a 'Chinese Parliament', a practice that is peculiar to the Regiment. In such a meeting anyone is free to offer suggestions or criticise the plan of action, regardless of rank or experience. It is a recognition that ordinary troopers within the SAS often possess considerable military experience, despite their lowly regimental rank. It also relates back to David Stirling's original thinking about the SAS: that it tolerates no sense of class. The team pored over maps of the MSR they were to watch. Like most highways, it was dotted with built-up areas. There were also four airfields and pumping stations for water in the area. They picked a location where the MSR was at its narrowest, a place midway between an airfield and the town of Banidahir, roughly 30km (18.5 miles) from each. Reaching that decision was relatively easy. The next one was how to get there – this was more difficult.

There were three ways to get to the destination: by walking, in Land Rover vehicles or by aircraft. Walking – tabbing – was discarded almost immediately. It would be impossible for each man to carry his equipment load over such a distance (each team member would be carrying over 100kg of kit – a back-breaking load). Land Rover insertion was not so lightly dismissed. There were several advantages. First, vehicles allowed a quick evacuation to be made in the event of being discovered or ambushed. Second, to travel in vehicles meant more firepower, such as General Purpose Machine Guns (GPMGs) and M19 40mm grenade launchers mounted on the vehicles themselves, could be taken into enemy territory. This would increase the firepower of the patrol significantly, as would the additional ammunition and explosives that could be carried on the vehicles. However, there were also disadvantages to using vehicles. First, and most importantly for a covert team, two vehicles substantially increased the danger of being compromised; after all, they make more noise and are bigger than a group of men, and thus more difficult to conceal (if it is dry they can also throw up clouds of dust). Second, the vehicles would undoubtedly need to be re-supplied with fuel. This would mean a Chinook helicopter flying in the replenishment, again risking the team being compromised. As they were going to stay in the location for at least a week, anything that increased the chances of being discovered was to be avoided. Third, the vehicles would have to be guarded at all times. If the team left them alone they might be discovered by the locals, who would then report them to the authorities, after which they might be booby-trapped by the enemy. To avoid this would mean at least one man staying with them at all times, thus reducing the overall effectiveness of the team. The third method of insertion was by aircraft, specifically the RAF's Chinook helicopter. This was

chosen for two reasons. First, it was the fastest way in which to get to the location. Second, the team would have had to be re-supplied by helicopter anyway, so why not fly in by chopper in the first place?

In his book, Ryan admits that it was a mistake to go in by helicopter. He now believes it would have been better to drive in and hide the vehicles under camouflage netting. In addition to the mobility and extra firepower that the Land Rovers would have given, the team would not have been saddled with the back-breaking loads they were forced to carry. However, the decision at the time was to leave the vehicles behind.

Scud-A had a range of 130km (81 miles) and was armed with a nuclear warhead

Having agreed on the method of insertion, the members of the team now had to decide how they would knock out the Scuds and landlines. This required examining in some detail the layout of the missile and its mobile launcher. Since the Gulf War the Scud has become an almost mythical weapon, and it has been accredited fearsome capabilities. The truth, as ever, is slightly different; indeed, the Iraqi missiles should not even be called Scuds.

Scud was the NATO codename for the Soviet R-17 short-range surface-to-surface missile. The initial SS-1 Scud-A had a range of 130km (81 miles), was armed with a nuclear warhead and was transported on an elevating launcher attached to the chassis of a modified Josef Stalin tank. The Scud-B and Scud-C followed, the latter having longer range and a wheeled launcher, though less accuracy than its predecessors. The

Above: An SAS Land Rover operating behind the lines in Iraq. 'Bravo Two Zero' decided to opt for a heliborne insertion into western Iraq, a decision that was to prove erroneous.

Scud-A and Scud-B versions were exported, to Egypt, Iraq, Libya, Syria and South Yemen. The missiles were delivered to these states with conventional warheads, though several, notably Iraq, have been developing chemical warheads. It was this potential that made the Iraqi Scuds much feared. The missile itself is a single-stage, liquid-cooled model, and has four fins to provide stabilisation and control. These supplement the control vanes at the nozzle end of the missile.

The Scud in Iraqi service is properly called the Al Husayn, and is slightly different compared with their Soviet counterparts. During the Iran-Iraq War both sides fired FROG (Free Rocket Over Ground) unguided artillery rockets at each other, plus Scuds. Iran periodically launched

Scuds against Iraqi cities, notably Kirkuk and Baghdad, but the Iraqis could not retaliate against Tehran, the Iranian capital, because of the distances involved. This was intolerable. Saddam Hussein therefore resolved to extend the range of his Scuds. With West German help he did just that, and by August 1987 the new missile, called Al Husayn, was ready. The original high-explosive warhead had been reduced in weight from 1000kg (2205lb) to 360kg (795lb), thereby boosting its range to 600km (375 miles). Between March and April 1988, over 180 were launched against Tehran and other cities.

The first Al Husayns were constructed from cannibalised Scuds, but then the Iraqis started building their own missiles. In the so-called Project 124, Iraq began to construct the missiles,

Below: Part of the massive Iraqi chemical arsenal that was discovered by UN inspectors after the war. The men of 'Bravo Two Zero' were concerned that Iraqi Scud warheads may have been armed with chemical agents.

again with West German help. Under the same project, Iraq tried to build a longer-range missile, codenamed Al Abbas. Test-launched in April 1988, it was apparently in production by the time the Gulf War broke out in 1990. Because of the secrecy that surrounded much of Iraq's space and ballistic weapons programmes, intelligence could not confirm how many Al Husayns and/or Scuds the Iraqis had (this is still unknown). However, there were thought to be between 200 and 1000 missiles, with 30-40 mobile launchers (American estimates before the war insisted that the Iraqis possessed only 18 launch vehicles, but this figure was quickly amended to 36 when the Gulf War broke out). The latter, called transporter-erector-launchers (TELs), travel with the missile stowed horizontally on a launcher arm that is raised to the vertical position off the rear of the vehicle for launch purposes.

Above: A column of Iraqi T-55 tanks. There were two Iraqi armoured divisions situated between the Saudi border and 'Bravo Two Zero's' first lying-up position, plus a host of enemy anti-aircraft batteries.

McNab and his men studied the information about the missiles and their launchers

---

The missiles themselves are very unsophisticated, having no guidance system of their own. The missile is 'guided' by the ground crew, who estimate the distance to the target and adjust the direction and elevation of the launcher. Realistically, the missile could be expected to land within a 3km (1.8-mile) radius of its target at the very most. This is why it is a weapon better employed against cities – they are large and difficult to miss (that said, of the total of 70 or more missiles that were launched against Saudi Arabia and Israel during the war, around 20 per cent failed to hit their targets). Nevertheless, as a weapon of terror it was very effective.

McNab and his men studied the information about the missiles and their launchers carefully. It soon became obvious that the men who prepared the missile for its launch were crucial players in the scene. TELs were usually escorted by a command vehicle carrying the commander and a surveyor. In the TEL itself were the crew (two in the front and the others in the back) with the missile command position in the centre of the TEL. The surveyor is the key player, for it is he that chooses the site and targets the missile. Once a site has been chosen, it takes approximately one hour of surveying, targeting and pumping propellants before the missile can be fired.

The SAS team talked about killing the TEL's crew. If the commander, surveyor and the TEL's command centre operators were killed it would obviously stop the launch of the missile. But they

SAS GULF WARRIORS

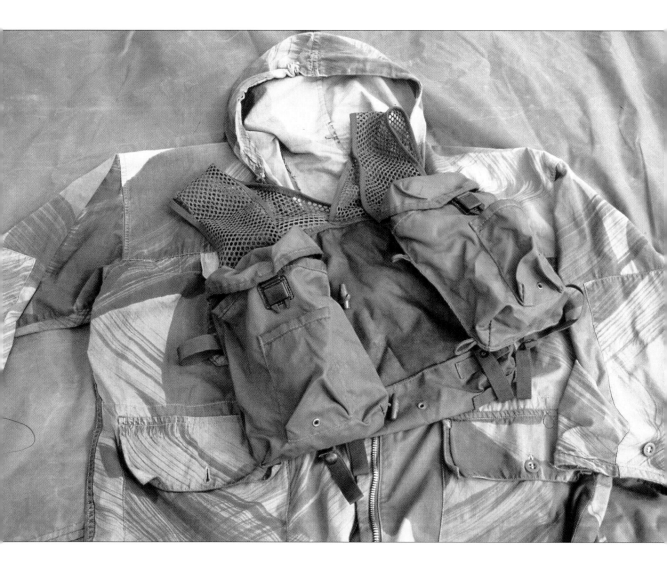

Above: SAS smock and chest webbing as worn by patrol members. It was to prove woefully inadequate in the freezing conditions encountered by the men in the desert.

could be replaced. What about calling down an air strike? In the popular imagination this is what the SAS did during the war, and to a certain extent the perception is correct. However, there were several problems with this. First, the missile might be fired before it could be hit from the air (again, contrary to popular opinion, there was not a Coalition warplane flying over every square kilometre of Iraq and Kuwait during every hour of the day during the war.) Second, the Regiment had not had the time to practise ground-to-air coordination of air attacks with the Americans. A member of the Regiment later lamented: 'By mid-December 1990 we had been rehearsing for every scenario, but the demand on other units to meet their own training package meant that we had little time to work up drills with American strike aircraft.'

There was another problem with regard to air strikes: the threat of being discovered by the Iraqis. The latter had very good direction-finding (DF) equipment: a series of listening posts around the country that provided bearings on radio sources. This meant they could target McNab and his team if they used the radio to call down an air strike. In McNab's words, they decided to use air strikes only 'if the Iraqis made us an offer we couldn't refuse – say, the world's supply of Scuds in convoy.'

Interestingly, neither McNab nor other SAS men who served behind the lines in the Gulf refer to taking laser designators with them on operations. There is a very good reason for this: the Regiment hardly used them, and none of the road watch patrols had them. The designators themselves are quite bulky and can weigh up to 20kg (44lb). McNab's team were already carrying over 100kg (220lb) per man; the last thing they needed was bulky, useless equipment.

Having earmarked air attacks to be used only in exceptional circumstances, 'Bravo Two Zero' decided to knock the Scuds out by destroying the control centre in the middle of the TEL. In this way the missile could not be launched. The missile itself was to be left well alone. The team did not want to blow up a missile that might contain chemical, biological or nuclear material (in its mad scramble to destroy the Scuds, the Coalition high command in Riyadh appears to have paid scant regard to aircraft destroying warheads potentially filled with agents of mass destruction; presumably better western Iraq to be laid waste than Israel).

What about the landlines? It was thought that the buried cables ran alongside the MSR and that every 10km or so there would be inspection manholes (this was yet another intelligence gap, which is really quite amazing considering that these landlines had been built with Western assistance). The team therefore decided to make four or six cuts along the cable and pack each with explosives, each timed to detonate at different times over a period of several days. The charges would be laid in one night, using small anti-personnel mines to booby trap the manholes. In this way it was hoped that the cable could be rendered useless over a six-day period.

Each man carried two weeks' supply of food and water, plus explosives and ammunition

Personal equipment was fairly standard, though tailored to the operation in hand. Each man carried two weeks' supply of food and water, plus explosives, ammunition and NBC clothing. The patrol had four tactical beacons (TACBEs) between them. These are standard pieces of kit, and can be used either as a beacon for search and rescue purposes, or as a radio. Bergens were also filled with spare batteries for the patrol radio, intravenous fluids and fluid-giving sets. A glaring omission was sleeping bags. These were left behind because the 'weather would not be too bad'. As two of the team, Sergeant Vince Phillips and Lance-Corporal Lane, later died of hypothermia during the mission, this decision was probably regretted. Nevertheless, even the best make mistakes, and weight considerations were uppermost in the men's minds. Each man also carried a basic first aid kit containing suture kit, pain killers, rehydrate, antibiotics and scalpel blades, plus two syrettes of morphine hung around the neck. Belt kit consisted of ammunition in pouches, water, emergency food, survival kit, shell dressings, knife and prismatic compass. As ever, the team carried the communal piss can.

Four of the team were armed with M16 assault rifles with 40mm grenade launchers

Other items of equipment issued to individuals included maps, though they were unsuited to the team's needs. In fact, they were designed for aircrews, and were therefore too small and showed few details. It is standard procedure to issue each team member with an escape map, but the ones the men initially received dated back to 1928! Fortunately, at the last minute the men were issued with up-to-date ones printed on silk.

Another item of kit were the indemnity notes given to each man. These were written in English and Arabic and promised £5000 to anyone who handed over a United Nations serviceman to a friendly power. Along the same lines, everyone carried 20 gold sovereigns to enable them to buy their way out of trouble or to facilitate a bribe. However, such measures did not work in the Gulf, and Allied airmen and soldiers who were captured were not able to buy their freedom. One suspects that though such inducements to the locals were undoubtedly appealing, the fear of aiding the enemy kept Iraqi civilians and soldiers firmly on the side of Saddam, and in any case, as mentioned above, the Iraqis them-

selves offered rewards for information leading to the whereabouts of Allied personnel in Iraq.

The team's choice of weapons was interesting. Four of the team were armed with M16 assault rifles with 40mm M203 grenade launchers. They carried 10 magazines of M16 ammunition (300 rounds) plus 200 rounds of Minimi ammunition. One weapon that was not carried by any patrol member was the SA-80 assault rifle. This small arm is held in contempt by the men of the Regiment, who consider it to be unreliable, prone to stoppages and of poor quality. The other four members of the patrol were armed with 5.56mm Minimi light machine guns and each carried 600 rounds of ammunition for their weapon. The weapons and equipment used by the SAS are studied in more detail in a later chapter, but suffice to say here that the Minimi is a versatile light machine gun, and a definite weight saving on the larger-calibre (7.62mm) GPMG also used by the regiment. That said, it has a rate of fire of 700-1000 rounds per minute. In any firefight, even using controlled bursts as employed by SAS soldiers, the patrol ammunition would soon be used up. This is in fact what happened to the team, and is one of the disadvantages associated with foot-mounted missions. In addition, each man also carried one 66mm M72 anti-tank weapon. They would have liked to have had more than one each, but again weight considerations and a shortage of these weapons ruled this out. Other weapons carried were grenades, including those for the M203 grenade launchers.

Interestingly, patrol members also put in a request for silenced pistols, which are quiet and deadly at close range. Though they have to be reloaded manually after a round is fired, they are exceptionally quiet. However, B Squadron was

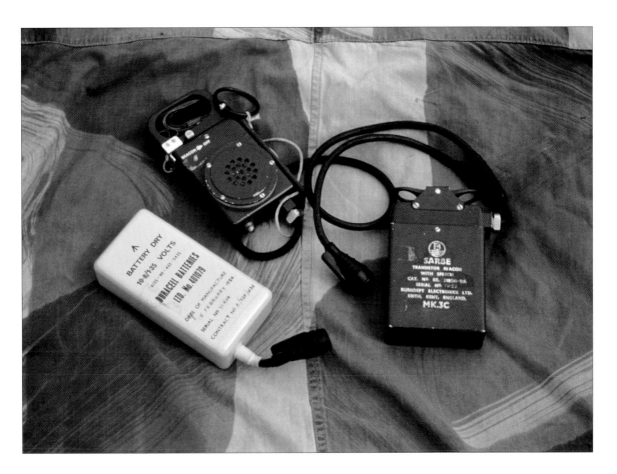

out of luck because there were none left in stores. However, these weapons were issued to members of the other SAS squadrons in the Gulf.

Mention should be made of the Claymore anti-personnel mines the team carried. Because of shortages these had to be fashioned by the men themselves from plastic boxes and nuts and bolts. This is an amazing state of affairs, and reflects badly upon British logistical efforts during the Gulf conflict.

There are other glaring anomalies with regard to equipment, and they reflect poorly on the logistical backup of the Regiment itself. For

Above: A surface-to-air rescue beacon, like the ones used in the Gulf. 'Bravo Two Zero' found them to be inadequate, because there were no aircraft close enough to pick up the signal.

example, Chris Ryan endeavoured to draw some cold-weather clothing from the stores before he left, only to be told by the squadron quartermaster sergeant that he was going to the desert and wouldn't need it as it 'won't be cold there.' In another incident before they left, Ryan relates how the patrol could not practice its contact drills because of a shortage of ammunition. Again, this is an unbelievable state of affairs.

Above: A Chinook helicopter comes in to land near Al Jouf. The team had a scare during the insertion, when an Iraqi anti-aircraft battery locked-on to the Chinook in which they were travelling and fired a surface-to-air missile. Fortunately, it missed.

The shortages did not only relate to ammunition. For one thing, there weren't any M203 grenades to be had anywhere. This problem was eventually solved when another member of the Regiment donated some to the patrol. Yet

another problem concerned the Land Rovers. Only A and D Squadrons had the 110 version. B Squadron was issued with short-wheelbased 90s, which had to be worked on to get them ready for cross-border operations. Thus the doors, tailgates, wing mirrors, windscreens and hessian tops were removed. However, such improvisation could not compensate for the lack of the proper vehicles. This obviously had a detrimental effect on the men's morale, as Chris Ryan states: 'it was pathetic trying to operate with the wrong equipment, and altogether our training was poor.'

All their plans and preparations complete, it was time to mount the mission. The first trip to the drop-off point was aborted due to the intensity of Allied air activity – there was no room in the air. This was fortuitous, for when they got back to Al Jouf the men started to strip their bergens of anything that was considered a luxury. In the words of Ryan, the weight of the bergens had reached silly proportions: 'the only way we could get them on was to sit down, settle the straps over our shoulders, and have a couple of the other guys pull us to our feet, as if they were hoisting knights on to their chargers.' Unfortunately, one of the items they discarded would be desperately needed in the days ahead: warm clothing.

The second journey to the drop-off point was uneventful enough, apart from a scare from an Iraqi Roland surface-to-air missile, which the Chinook pilot managed to avoid. When the men were on the ground, though, it was a different story. First of all they were surprised by the amount of activity there was in their area. Eventually they found a lying-up position (LUP) in a cave located near the MSR. But then they failed to establish radio contact with the SAS's forward operating base. This in itself was not a disaster, as the men could go back to the landing site at their pre-arranged time and rendezvous with the Chinook, and there exchange radios. However, it was a foretaste of things to come.

'We might as well have sighted our LUP in the middle of Piccadilly Circus'

The first detailed reconnaissance of the area they were in revealed that 'Bravo Two Zero' was at its correct position, but that it was also in the middle of a populated area with plantations to the north and south, and an enemy anti-aircraft battery to the northwest of its LUP. As McNab himself states: 'From a tactical point of view, we might as well have sited our LUP in the middle of Piccadilly Circus.' To increase the difficulty of this initial situation still further, more enemy troops arrived and located themselves 300m (330 yards) from the patrol's position. It was obvious to the patrol that they would have to be evacuated straight away. However, attempts to talk to Al Jouf via the PRC319 radio came to nought. In fact, the team had been given the wrong frequencies – an amazing blunder that was to cost the lives of three of the patrol.

The first day of monitoring the MSR brought disaster: they were discovered by a boy tending a herd of goats. The patrol members tried to make it to the sanctuary of the Syrian border. In a series of desperate firefights and contacts with the enemy the SAS team used up all their ammunition. Nevertheless, the men acquitted themselves well, and the surviving team members estimated that they killed over 250 enemy soldiers in the firefights during their flight. When it is considered that the Iraqis deployed armoured personnel carriers against the SAS team, this is a phenomenal casualty rate, and also a superb testament to the weapons training of the Regiment.

He discovered that his blisters had burns, the skin was raw and bleeding

Ryan's words about the battles with the Iraqis separates the reality from the myth regarding SAS men, and are worth repeating here: 'If anyone say he's not frightened in a firefight, I don't believe him. I was shit-scared, and so was everyone else. I know the SAS has a high reputation, but the guys are not superhuman: they may have enormous courage, but they are subject to the same fear as anyone else. The regiment's strength lies in the fact that its members are highly trained to control their fear and respond positively to whatever threat they are facing.'

The tab to the border involved crossing 120km (75 miles) of harsh terrain, which was made all the worse by the freezing weather. All efforts to raise assistance via the TACBEs failed – the men were on their own. By this time the whole of the area was alerted to their presence, and soldiers and civilians eagerly hunted for the Western troops. The immediate concern of the team, though, was the weather. The rain, sleet and snow that lashed them was severely reducing their chances of survival. Dehydration and hypothermia became greater enemies than the Iraqi troops themselves.

As the team scrambled west the inevitable happened: the group got separated. One man, Sergeant Vince Phillips, died of hypothermia and general exhaustion in the snow-lashed hills. Another was captured, while a third, Corporal Chris Ryan, embarked on an epic lone journey that took him to Syria. He eventually walked more than 300km (225 miles) in total during the course of his escape and evasion. His description of his flight is certainly gripping, but it is also indicative of the mental and physical toughness of SAS soldiers. By the third night on the run from his pursuers, for example, he was physically exhausted and alone. The next dawn he managed to find a hiding place among some rocks, giving him an opportunity to examine his feet. He discovered that his blisters had burns, the skin was raw and bleeding and his toenails were lifting. At this stage it had been five days since he had eaten a proper meal. Three days later, and after drinking poisoned water, Ryan's teeth were loose, his gums were bleeding, his feet and hands were cut to ribbons and smelt due to infection. Nevertheless, he continued with his journey and reached Syria after seven nights and eight days.

He had eaten nothing aside from two small packets of biscuits, as well as having virtually nothing to drink. The effects on his body were brutal, such as a severe loss of weight. It was two weeks before he could walk properly again, six weeks before sensation returned to his fingers and toes, and he had a severe blood disorder and

liver problems due to drinking water from a source near a uranium-processing plant.

The other five initially fared better. They managed to reach the Iraqi town of Al Qaim, which was near the Syrian border, but then their luck started to run out. Their presence was discovered by the Iraqis, who gave chase. Throughout the confusion the SAS men got separated again, this time into one group of three and one of two. The enemy began to close in. To make matters

Above: An Iraqi Scud missile leaves its mobile launcher and heads for Israel. The SAS road watch patrols were part of the effort to track down the Scuds. However, the teams were hastily prepared and launched, and suffered accordingly.

worse, the men by this stage had used up all their ammunition and had thrown away their weapons. Members of the Regiment are trained in the use of foreign weapons. In theory this means they can use the enemy's firearms when conducting missions behind the lines. However, such a scenario is more pertinent to a counter-insurgency operation, i.e. a long-term mission behind the lines. McNab and his men wanted to get away from their pursuers as fast as possible.

Trooper Robert Consiglio was killed at this time, and McNab and his companion were captured soon afterwards. That left the two remaining members of the patrol. They managed to evade the Iraqis for a short while longer. However, one of them, Lance-Corporal 'Legs' Lane, was in a desperate state and died of hypothermia, and his companion was captured. The military exploits of 'Bravo Two Zero' had ended.

McNab was subject to a mock execution as the Iraqis tried to make him confess

Capture brought fresh perils for those who had been caught. Initially all went well for the SAS soldiers, who were separated for interrogation. The Iraqis asked each man for the 'Big Four': name, rank, serial number and date of birth. As this is permissible under the Geneva Convention the men gave them. However, the Iraqis wanted to know a lot more. An interpreter asked McNab what religion he was. He told them he was Church of England. However, they wanted him to admit he was Jewish. The interrogators were particularly keen to link them all with Israel. When McNab and his men started to say the things the Iraqis did not want to hear, he was beaten severely.

The SAS men tried to deceive the Iraqis, such as telling them they were from a search and rescue unit, but that only resulted in more beatings. Humiliations and more beatings followed, and

McNab was subject to a mock execution as the Iraqis tried to make him confess to being an Israeli commando. If he had done so, then he would have undoubtedly been paraded on Iraqi television, where he would have been forced to repeat his 'confession'. Some of the Iraqi questions bordered on the sheer ludicrous. For example, the interrogators repeatedly insisted that McNab was Jewish. In a final effort to persuade his tormentors he was not, he informed them that he was uncircumcised, and proceeded to show them that this was so. This caused much hilarity among his captors.

The relief was not to last long, however, for soon there were more beatings and vicious interrogation sessions for all of them. Inevitably, the soldiers' bodies began to get seriously ill. When they were finally released after more than a month of brutality, they were all very ill. One of the patrol members had a serious foot wound, but throughout his captivity had received no treatment for it. As a result his foot swelled to the size of a marrow, though this did not stop the guards giving him further beatings, mainly concentrated on his bad foot.

The amazing thing is that the members of the patrol who were captured survived their ordeal. This was undoubtedly due to their physical fit-

ness, allied to their mental strength. What comes across most strongly when reading McNab's book is that he kept his mind working even during the beatings, trying to think of ways to appease his interrogators and spin out time without actually providing any information. At the end of the day the Iraqis, for all their brutality,

Above: An American F/A-18 Hornet over western Iraq. Despite the intensity of the air effort to search out Scuds, the results were poor. The launchers were difficult to find, not least because the Iraqis proved adept at concealing them.

failed to get the SAS soldiers to say what they wanted them to say.

Ultimately those who had been captured were returned by the Iraqis after the cessation of hostilities. For those who had survived, plus Chris Ryan who had made it back on his own, the subsequent months were difficult. Each man was filled with different emotions as he tried to get back to 'normal' following his ordeal. For some, such as Chris Ryan, there were feelings of guilt. Recovering from trauma, even for élite soldiers, takes time, and can put an immense strain on individuals and their families. Even SAS soldiers suffer from post-traumatic stress.

As an interesting footnote, when Chris Ryan returned to Al Jouf he discovered that B Squadron had been provided with tents and that the organisation side of things was much better. It was a shame that it could not have been so when the team set off.

Far more serious had been the inadequate maps, and the lack of intelligence

---

The failure of the patrol led to a lot of questions being asked at Stirling Lines after the war had ended, questions concerning the Regiment's operating procedures and its logistics set up. Though there had been shortages of equipment and ammunition, the general consensus among patrol members themselves was that these things had not contributed to 'Bravo Two Zero's' ultimate failure. Far more serious had been the inadequate maps, and the lack of intelligence concerning the nature of the terrain they were being inserted into (the men were expecting to be landed into sandy terrain, into which they could dig to build observation posts, not a rocky landscape). By way of a cruel irony, the accurate intelligence the patrol did receive was useless to them. For example, the men demanded to see satellite imagery of the area they were being inserted into. At first there were none to be had, but persistent requests and demands eventually succeeded in some arriving. However, they were of extremely poor quality, and appeared to show that the operational area was very flat and open. This made the team quite happy because it confirmed the wisdom of leaving the Land Rovers behind (in flat terrain anything large, such as vehicles, can be seen for great distances, to say nothing of the dust clouds they would kick up). Unfortunately, the men's interpretation was completely wrong. What they had failed to realise, due to lack of tuition as to how to interpret satellite imagery, was that they were reading the transparencies upside down.

In addition, the TACBEs were revealed to be seriously deficient, and therefore should not have been relied upon to provide backup communications. The fact that the patrol had been given the wrong radio frequencies was a mistake, but it did illustrate the need to tighten up mission planning in general.

If there were lessons to learn, there were also reasons for the SAS as a whole to be pleased with its procedures. Once again, the weapons training given to SAS soldiers had shown itself to be highly effective. The casualties suffered by the enemy during contacts with a small number of men illustrated that the Regiment's contact drills are just right (notwithstanding that the team members had inadequate ammunition to practice them at base before they were inserted). In addition, the Regiment's escape and evasion drills, as used by Chris Ryan on his epic journey, proved themselves to be spot on.

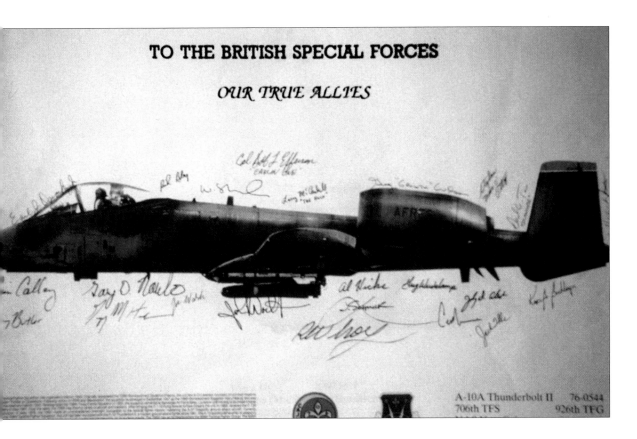

TO THE BRITISH SPECIAL FORCES

OUR TRUE ALLIES

A-10A Thunderbolt II   76-0544
706th TFS   926th TFG

Above: In recognition of their sterling work performed on the ground, and the self-sacrifice of teams such as 'Bravo Two Zero', signed artworks such as the above were presented to the Regiment by US Air Force units.

Perhaps what the mission illustrated above all is that, at the end of the day, SAS soldiers are only human like everyone else. They may be highly trained, but they can also make simple mistakes. For example, Chris Ryan decided not to take water-purification tablets with him, believing that he would be drinking from jerrycans. He knew that the team would not be taking water from wells for fear of them being poisoned. What he didn't realise was that he would be drinking from the Euphrates during his flight. In hindsight it appears a glaring omission, but we are all wiser with the benefit of hindsight.

Although the mission was ultimately a failure, it has left a lasting testimony to the physical and mental standards of members of the Regiment. Their ordeal has naturally left scars, notably the antipathy the patrol members felt towards their captors. McNab summed up the consensus of opinion when he said that if he met his captors in the street and thought he could get away with it, he would 'slot them'. Whatever the rights and wrongs of such a stance, he and the other members of the patrol can take pride in the fact that their conduct was a credit to the SAS.

CHAPTER 6

Scud Hunting

In an effort to destroy the Iraqi Scuds before they dragged Israel into the war and fractured the Coalition, A and D Squadrons, 22 SAS, were unleashed on western Iraq. The Regiment's mobile fighting columns raced into enemy territory and began the systematic hunting down and destroying of Saddam's missiles. The weather conditions were sometimes awful, and there were often savage contacts with the enemy, but the SAS got the job done.

The failure of the road watch patrols did not significantly affect the SAS's effort in western Iraq. They were, after all, just one strand of the Regiment's overall strategy. There were still the fighting columns and the operations against the concealed landlines to come. This chapter discusses the SAS mobile fighting columns that roamed western Iraq, and compares them to the American efforts to combat the Scuds that took place farther north.

Whereas B Squadron had undertaken the road watches, it was the turn of A and D Squadrons to mount the mobile columns. The Regiment gathered together its vehicles at its forward base at Al Jouf and assembled its columns. Each one would consist of approximately 12 Land Rover vehicles plus motorcycle outriders. The vehicles, in true SAS tradition, were heavily armed. The Land Rovers bristled with GPMGs, 40mm M19 grenade launchers, Milan anti-tank weapons and Stinger surface-to-air missiles (SAMs). In addition, most of the weapons had thermal imaging night sights (passive infra-red sensors that convert detected heat into video images – used mainly for night work), and the drivers wore night vision goggles.

There were four columns in all: two from A Squadron and two from D Squadron. Contrary to popular opinion, the SAS was not free to roam

Opposite: The crew of an SAS Land Rover pose for a family shot behind the lines in Iraq. Note the Milan anti-tank missile launcher in the background.

Above: The time before a mission is always tense. All the briefings have been given, all the equipment has been checked, all that is left is each man with his thoughts – thoughts of home and loved ones far away.

wherever it wanted. General Norman Schwarz-kopf's SOCCENT had conferred with the Joint Special Operations Command and Washington to divide western Iraq into three areas. Colonel Massey and his SAS soldiers were to patrol the southern 'box', which straddled the Amman-Baghdad highway. The other two areas lay along the Syrian border, one being located near the town of Shab al Hiri, while the other lay near the town of Al Qaim, farther northeast. Clearing

these two boxes would be the responsibility of the Americans, specifically the élite Delta Force. For this purpose a base was established at Ar Ar, located in northern Saudi Arabia some 50km (31 miles) from the Iraqi border. From there Delta Force could launch operations against the two northern boxes. After the disappointment of the cancellation of its hostage-rescue mission, Delta Force was delighted to have been given another task. It was also an opportunity to improve the unit's somewhat tarnished image among the special forces brotherhood.

In the first few days of the war the Coalition believed that the majority of the Scuds being fired against Israel were from Iraqi bases numbered H1, H2 and H3 (see map on page 189). The Coalition had targeted these bases from the beginning of the air war. For example, H2 and H3 were hit by US Air Force aircraft on the night of 16/17 January, and on the next night it was the turn of US Navy jets. Nevertheless, the Israelis were not satisfied. To the horror of the Coalition, they were planning their own strikes. They would hit the area with their own jets, they informed the Americans, and would land their own troops in the area to hunt the Scuds. Frantic messages went to Israel from the Americans: we are doing all we can to destroy the Scuds, please do not use your own forces. For

the moment, at least, the Israelis were appeased. But how long would their restraint last?

In Riyadh it was realised that speed was critical. Therefore, the first SAS mobile columns started on 20 January. But they were not just hunting Scuds. Iraq had deployed hundreds of artillery pieces and multiple launch rocket systems capable of firing chemical warheads. They had a range of 30-40km (18.5-25 miles), which

Below: Special forces operations rely on timely and accurate intelligence for success. Therefore, American and British aerial photographs were crucial to the SAS regarding the Regiment's area of operations in western Iraq.

Right: An Iraqi Free Rocket Over Ground (FROG) artillery rocket, some of which were also targeted by SAS columns in Iraq. With their ability to fire chemical warheads as well as high-explosive rounds, they were a potent threat to UN units.

meant they could hit Allied units in Saudi Arabia. And the Iraqis were quite capable of using them. During the war with Iran, for example, Iraqi units had fired many chemical artillery shells during the 1988 offensive in the Fao peninsula. This was re-iterated in the US Army's *Desert Shield Order of Battle Handbook*, which was issued to all US military personnel in the Gulf: 'Once authorization for chemical weapons use is given, corps commanders are given chemical rounds to be delivered by artillery. Chemical warheads include three types: a lethal mustard agent, an incapacitating agent, and tear gas.' The SAS teams were ordered to knock out the battlefield chemical weapons delivery systems, as and when they found them.

When the invasion failed to materialise, the SAS columns pressed deeper into Iraq

The first day, 20 January, was uneventful, partly because the SAS limited its incursion into enemy territory to 40km (25 miles) into Iraq. This was because the Israelis had threatened to invade the area, and no one in the Regiment wanted to be killed by Israeli jets. When the invasion failed to materialise, the SAS columns pressed deeper into Iraq. The urgency of the mission had been increased: on 22 January a Scud hit Tel Aviv, killing three civilians. On the next day yet another was launched at Israel, though fortunately it fell into an uninhabited area. These launches did

nothing to appease the Israelis, who were itching to send in their own forces.

In desperation, Lieutenant-General Charles Horner and Brigadier-General 'Buster' Glosson, chief targeter and commander of all US Air Force wings in the Gulf, hatched a plan for all the combat aircraft available to the Allies – some 2000 warplanes – to be diverted to western Iraq.

In a three-day campaign, the UN aircraft would completely flatten the area, particularly around Al Qaim, Rutba and other population centres. The enemy targets that faced destruction included police stations, service areas, and anything else that could support Scud operations. Also, bombers would sow mines on all the roads and destroy over 60 underpasses (these were favourite Scud hiding places). The plan was presented to Schwarzkopf, who rejected it for two reasons. First, it would result in the deaths of many civilians; and second, it would not shorten the war. In any case, by this time General Dynamics F-16 Fighting Falcons and Fairchild Republic A-10 Thunderbolt IIs had been diverted to the Scud hunt, and it was felt that more aircraft would just

Above: An American AWACS on the ground at Dhahran air base. Such aircraft provided the link between SAS fighting columns on the ground in Iraq and UN aircraft in the skies over enemy territory, albeit often not quickly enough.

result in more crowded skies, with no tangible results with regard to destroying Scuds.

Back on the ground in Iraq, the SAS initially had mixed fortunes. Its columns had not seen any Scud launchers for three days, and the men were getting frustrated, especially since another missile had been launched against Israel on 23 January (though fortunately it caused no casualties). However, on 23 January the Regiment had a stroke of luck. One of A Squadron's columns was operating between Nukhayb and Karbala, southwest of Baghdad, when the men ran into a group of four Iraqis driving across the desert. In

a brief firefight three of the Iraqis were killed. The fourth was captured and interrogated. Being highly relieved that he was not going to be killed by the SAS soldiers, he began to impart some valuable information. This took the form of a map he was carrying, which detailed the positions of a previously unseen enemy brigade in western Iraq. The SAS soldiers immediately relayed this information to the Tactical Air Co-Ordination Centre, and within a few hours the brigade was being pounded by Coalition aircraft.

On 24 January the SAS began to push ever deeper into the 'Scud box'. Now the SAS soldiers began to encounter the enemy more, and there were frequent violent contacts. Whenever possible, SAS attacks were launched against the enemy at night. A Squadron itself suddenly became very busy:

'We had spotted the launcher two days earlier and had followed it, travelling at night over rough terrain until we had caught up with it and managed to plant explosives on it. The blast shattered the night's silence and sent a mushroom of flame high into the sky as our charges detonated, crippling the target and giving us the signal to kick off at anything that moved around the site.'

The SAS teams had been fully briefed as to the threat of Iraqi chemical weapons

---

In the cold light of day the men discovered that it was not a Scud but a FROG surface-to-surface unguided artillery rocket. The two systems look very similar: the FROG has a cylindrical body, a conical nose and four large control fins. Ominously, Soviet FROGs were usually armed with nuclear warheads, and, as ever, they could also be armed with chemical warheads. No one knew what the Iraqi warheads contained, but the worst scenario was feared. From their lying-up position (LUP), the SAS soldiers recognised the smaller rocket on its launcher, but no matter – they would destroy it: 'Scud or FROG, it had the capability to hit Allied targets and that was all that mattered to us.'

The SAS teams had been fully briefed as to the threat of Iraqi chemical weapons, but they had to take a chance and knock the missile out, chemical warhead or not. This contrasts sharply with 'Bravo Two Zero', which specifically avoided damaging enemy missile warheads through fear of their contents – though the FROGs could not hit Israel (they were battlefield weapons), they could inflict damage on Allied units waiting for the ground offensive in Saudi Arabia.

A lot has been written about the Iraqi chemical threat, but how great was it? As far as is known (and even today no one knows for sure), Iraq possessed, and possesses, all the main military chemical agents. These include blood agents, such as hydrogen cyanide, which disrupt the ability of the blood to absorb oxygen; blister agents, such as mustard, which cause skin burns and inflammation of the mucous membranes; and nerve agents, such as Sarin, which disrupt the central nervous system and thus vital involuntary muscular activities, like circulation and respiration. With hindsight we know that the Iraqi commanders on the ground had no intention of using chemical weapons, but this was known at the time by neither the Coalition High Command in Riyadh nor the SAS in Iraq.

Despite the fact that they had immobilised the launcher with charges, the SAS soldiers from A Squadron stayed where they were. 'Nothing was said when the explosion erupted; it's not like in the movies where the good guys all stand around cheering.' Like many contacts between the Iraqis and the SAS, the special forces soldiers were often forced to fight off Iraqi attacks. So it was this time. But, as on so many occasions, bluff and audacity saved the day:

Special forces troops need above-average weapon skills, and must hit what they aim at

---

'Depending on the professionalism of the ragheads, they may have spotted us and mounted an anti-ambush operation, so we stayed low and quiet until it was clear what was happening and that our position had not been compromised in any way. Almost a minute later several trucks appeared from the rear of the site, all full of ragheads as they abandoned their position and tried to leg it.'

The one thing that is inadvisable when confronting the SAS is to present yourself as a target. Special forces troops have above-average weapons skills, and usually hit what they aim at: 'They were about 300m [330 yards] away and without delay we cracked off a couple of 66s [M72 66mm anti-tank weapons].' What the SAS soldiers had not realised was that there were several enemy trucks and armoured personnel carriers that lay undiscovered. They were about 100m (110 yards) from the FROG launcher, and had not been spotted by the team that had crept for-

Below: SAS motorcycle outriders behind the lines in Iraq. Though SAS Mobility Troops had experimented with such machines for years before the Gulf War, the conflict in Arabia was the first in which they used motorbikes in anger.

ward in the darkness to lay the charges. They now appeared, and around 150 Iraqi soldiers faced an eight-man SAS team. However, cool professionalism took over, and the SAS soldiers followed their drills exactly. First priority was to disable the first and last truck in the convoy:

'As far as we were concerned the Iraqi rank and file were a bunch of thick ragheads'

'We banjoed the front and rear vehicles at the same time, but they had at least three armoured personnel carriers and they quickly opened up on us. The thud of their heavy calibre weapons seemed to get louder, probably because the rounds were ripping into the ground just in front of us. We knew we were on to a hiding, but the ragheads must have thought we were a much bigger unit. To our surprise they just raced away as quick as they could.'

The firefight had been fierce but short-lived – probably just a couple of minutes – and all that was left were two smouldering trucks. The SAS soldiers wasted no time. They left their LUP and sought their vehicles. Then they were away. As was standard operating procedure (SOP), they wanted to put as much space between themselves and the enemy as possible:

'It was essential to move fast. As far as we were concerned the Iraqi rank and file were a bunch of thick ragheads, but many of their officers had trained in the West, even at Sandhurst, prior and during the Iran-Iraq War. They were aware of British tactics, and while we didn't think they had the balls, there was a possibility that they could turn around and ambush us during the day. If that happened we could have been well

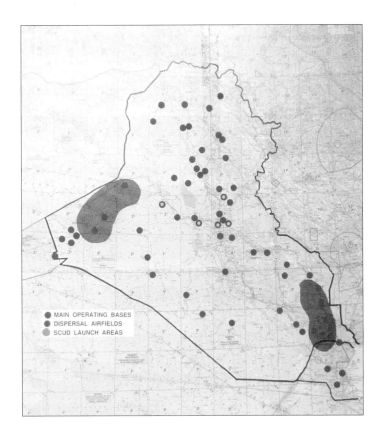

Above: An American intelligence map showing the main Iraqi airfields and bases during the Gulf conflict. Note the shaded area in western Iraq, where the SAS fighting columns, and Delta Force, operated against Scud launcher columns.

MAIN OPERATING BASES
DISPERSAL AIRFIELDS
SCUD LAUNCH AREAS

once again the 336th TFS rendered it useless. The Coalition special forces were beginning to gain the upper hand, and the scales were tipped further in their favour by the arrival of Delta Force's 1st Squadron at King Fahd International Airport on 1 February 1991.

The American élite unit was then rushed north to Ar Ar, from where it would be sent into the northern 'Scud box' to hunt for the Iraqi missiles. The man responsible for Delta Force's operations, Major-General Wayne Downing, head of the US Joint Special Operations Command at Fort Bragg, went to see the SAS commander in Riyadh, Colonel Massey, about Delta Force's operations. Massey briefed Downing about the difficulties his men would face in Iraq. In particular, he warned him about the Bedouins, who would undoubtedly report the presence of any teams to the Iraqis. Nevertheless, Downing was confident his men could perform just as well as the SAS (to get these men into Iraq, Delta Force had the services of Task Force 160, a helicopter unit that flew Sikorsky CH-53 Sea Stallion, Boeing Vertol CH-47 Chinook and Sikorsky UH-60 Black Hawk helicopters in a number of special operations variants).

When Delta Force was in the theatre, Massey's words proved to be true. Near Al Qaim there were many Bedouins, and they reported the American presence to the Iraqis. Very soon the American élite troops found themselves under attack. In early February, for example, nine Iraqi

and truly fucked.' Fortunately the Iraqis did not pursue them, and the men were able to make good their escape.

As January came to an end, the Regiment had more success. A fighting column spotted two Scud convoys and ordered in an air strike. The Americans obliged, and several F-15E Eagles from the US Air Force's 336th Tactical Fighter Squadron destroy the convoys totally. In addition, the SAS also spotted a Scud launch site:

armoured vehicles pursued a Delta Force patrol across the desert. The special forces were on foot and would have been mown down were it not for the fact that an F-15 Eagle appeared and scattered the enemy. Then US helicopters managed to pick the men up. Two days later, another Delta Force team was chased by Iraqi helicopters, being saved only by the appearance of another Eagle, which destroyed one helicopter and chased off the rest. Though Delta Force had a tough time of it, its missions in Iraq made a valuable contribution towards the Scud hunt, as well as repairing Delta Force's reputation.

By the end of January the Regiment's activities had provoked a vigorous response

So pleased was Schwarzkopf with Delta Force's performance that he allowed another Delta Force squadron and an Army Ranger company to be deployed to Ar Ar. This meant the number of men operating in Iraq could be increased, and there were eventually over 200 US élite troops in Mesopotamia. Though the number of confirmed Scud kills was small, Delta Force's efforts did limit the launcher teams' endeavours. With the aid of Eagles, Delta sowed hundreds of Gator mines on roads, underpasses and other suspected concealment sites. In this way the Scud launchers were forced into areas that could be more easily watched. But what of the SAS?

By the end of January the Regiment's activities had provoked a vigorous Iraqi response. On 29 January, for example, the Iraqis attacked an SAS column, damaging two of the latter's vehicles beyond repair, although losing 10 dead and three of their own vehicles in the process. One SAS soldier was also badly wounded, but was evacuated to Saudi Arabia and survived the war. From 30 January to 3 February the SAS was extremely active in 'Scud Alley'. On the latter date an SAS team from 1 and 17 Troops ordered an air strike on a Scud convoy. This preceded a prolonged contact, when it was realised that the aircraft had destroyed only one of the launchers. The SAS attacked the rest with their vehicle-mounted Milans, scoring a direct hit on a Scud missile and its launcher. However, the Iraqis counterattacked and drove off the SAS, though not before the latter had ordered a further air attack that destroyed most of the convoy.

Most of the SAS patrols that were operating in western Iraq at this time were vehicle-mounted, but not all. Some patrols were also sent in on foot, as a member of D Squadron relates:

'We had clocked up four patrols into Iraq and the squadron had bagged about a dozen targets, but there was no time to relax. The pressure was increasing from Riyadh for more success, and just as soon as we had been debriefed and re-supplied we were back on the road. Some of the mobile teams had already chalked up their Scud scores by painting silhouettes of the launchers on the wings of their Land Rovers.

'The mission was simple: find the two launchers and mallet them'

'US intelligence had monitored recent launcher activity in our sector, and after just 12 hours back inside Saudi we were preparing to attend another operational briefing, at which the Americans would outline full details of the potential targets they had tracked. We were to fly into Iraq and

check out two areas identified by the US Air Force as "Iraqi operational sites" and eliminate both by means of the explosives we would be carrying, or by calling down air strikes. The briefing was followed by an O Group, which was headed by our boss [troop commander] and the squadron commander. The mission was simple: find the two launchers and mallet them by whatever means possible and then fuck off out of the area as quickly as possible. The sector was believed to be alive with Republican Guard units transmitting through the region en route to reinforce Iraqi forces in and around Kuwait.

'After a night's sleep we packed our bergens and prepared our kit for another move into the

Above: An SAS night firing drill. In western Iraq the shooting skills of the Regiment were responsible for many patrols driving off much larger Iraqi formations with heavy losses. Where possible, though, firefights were avoided.

field. For the trip we made sure we all carried tubes of ant-killer. The little bastards had earlier bitten us to bits, and came close to being more of a threat than the Scuds. I always shit myself when it comes to helicopter insertion – the actual point of drop-off is always the most dangerous, and you always think you're going to get bumped – but this time we were OK.

'Using the nearest MSR, which as I recall was to our right, as our key reference point, we

Above: A heavily laden SAS Land Rover in wet conditions behind enemy lines. The SAS found that western Iraq at the beginning of 1991 was cold and wet, and the frequent low cloud often curtailed Allied air activity.

tabbed out of the area to a new location. Here we were able to put in an OP on the road while resting up for the next move. Moving across such open terrain was made easier due to GPS [Global Positioning System].'

As ever, the weather and terrain had a debilitating effect on the men:

'At dawn I remember seeing several jets flying low overhead, probably on a photo-reconnaissance of the area to examine the damage we had inflicted the night before. At this point we had been in the field for just four days, and to be honest we were knackered. It was a cold morning. The sky was overcast, and I remember being surprised to see aircraft flying in such weather.'

Contrary to popular opinion, the desert is not always scorching hot; in fact, western Iraq in early 1991 was particularly cold: 'What really bothered us was the drop in temperature; it was so cold I had a bet with a mate over whether it would rain or snow.'

'The first thing to go off your back in a contact is your bergen'

One of the most important aspects of operating behind enemy lines is re-supply. Food and ammunition can be quickly used up by élite teams, and without proper logistical support a mission can be fatally compromised:

'Sleep and food are the most important things, and we had had little of either. We had cached a lot of our food on day two. This is SOP when you are operating in such a big area and need a reserve of stores at a later date. It also allows the team to cover more ground without carrying so much weight.'

A cache is also useful if the team is bumped by the enemy, because everyone is aware of where it is. While evading the enemy, team members know where there is a source of supply:

'The first thing to go off your back in a contact is your bergen, leaving you with minor supplies in your belt. Thus the cache is very important, although if you run with no GPS to locate the area you're probably fucked anyway.'

SAS field rations are basic. Liberal quantities of chocolate ('the best buzz food') are always carried to provide instant energy. The soldiers themselves also carry 'hexy blocks': small, white tablets of hexamine fuel that burn well but without smell. However, they can only be used in daylight – the flames can be seen at night – and during the day they are dug into the ground to avoid any chance of being spotted. These tiny fires are ideal for cooking food and boiling water, and instead of the square standard-issue mess tins, the majority of SAS soldiers carry old '44-issue water bottles, which have a metal mug fitted to their base. The mugs are used to boil water, with a tin of food being boiled inside the mug. The can is then pierced and the food eaten, with tea or coffee added to the remaining water for a hot brew. Masking tape is usually secured around the top edge of the mug to prevent lips being burnt. In addition, the hot water can be poured directly into boil-in-the-bag rations. A second mug of water may also be used to make a curry, though this depends on the area in which the patrol is operating, for smell can easily compromise a team. Often, though, because the men are too near the enemy, food will be eaten cold.

Despite the Coalition air activity, the Iraqis were often very careless and sloppy. An SAS foot patrol from D Squadron came across a Scud convoy in early February:

'Through our scope we couldn't believe what we were seeing'

'We had just been on the comms net arranging a re-supply for the following morning to bring in more ammunition and food when we heard the distinctive sound of a convoy nearby, but nobody could see anything. We were desperate for ammunition, particularly 66mm LAWs, and our immediate thoughts were that we would have to abandon our position.'

Right: An abandoned Iraqi anti-aircraft gun. There were many such pieces manned by enemy anti-aircraft units in western Iraq in early 1991, and they posed a large threat to the SAS teams operating there, especially the foot patrols.

The team was well camouflaged ('out of sight among the rocky scrapes we had made') and its members just sat and watched. Before long the Iraqis came into sight late in the afternoon. It was a sizeable target in the form of 'a column of about 25 vehicles in all, including two Scud launchers. In the main they were BMPs [Soviet-built infantry fighting vehicles] and BRDMs [Soviet-built armoured reconnaissance patrol vehicles], and they had all pulled into the side of the MSR.'

The SAS soldiers could not believe their luck; 'It appeared that one of the Scud launchers had broken down. Several mechanics or fitters were trying to sort out the problem while the vehicle crews stood smoking beside the road. As we monitored the situation through our scopes we couldn't believe what we were seeing.' The Iraqis made no attempt to pull any camouflage netting over their vehicles, they just parked them up on the side of the road in the open. They were a sitting duck. And yet the SAS team could do little by itself:

This was an opportunity for Uncle Sam to earn some brownie points

'Any question of mounting an attack was a non-starter. We were short of ammunition and would stand little chance against such a heavily armed unit. This was an opportunity for Uncle Sam to earn some brownie points and blitz the convoy.'

One of the reasons the SAS is so successful is that its members can realistically appraise a situation: 'If we tried to take them on, it could have been "game over" for us, and the prospect of being taken prisoner did not appeal to any of us,

for the simple reason that we knew the Iraqis would ignore the Geneva Convention when it came to special forces.' (The Geneva Convention regarding the treatment of prisoners of war makes provision for the humane treat-ment of captured service personnel. The convention gives prisoners certain rights, such as to be kept in a place of safety, to be given medical care when necessary, and to have access to food and water. A prisoner is also allowed to keep

items of sentimental value, and is entitled to a receipt for any other personal items like money that is taken from him; prisoners are also allowed to write letters. All these provisions were blatantly ignored by the Iraqis.) One SAS soldier was particularly succinct when it came to the prospect of surrender:

'All we were required to give was the "Big Four" – name, rank, number and age – but the moment they put a scalpel near my bollocks I

Left: An Iraqi tank is turned into scrap metal. When SAS teams spotted worthwhile targets, the procedure was to call down an air strike on them. Failing that, the SAS Land Rovers would engage the targets themselves with their Milans, from as far away as possible to minimise risks.

an air attack. For some of the men this was the first time they would witness a combat air patrol strike up close: 'I had only ever seen one from a distance in the past, during training in Scotland, but the attack would take place less than 500m [545 yards] from our position.' The message was passed back to the SAS's forward base, then to American AWACS aircraft, who passed the targeting details on to the Eagles loitering over western Iraq. By this stage of the war the F-15Es were armed with GBU-12 laser-guided bombs, which were deadly effective, and recent research has shown that the Coalition's 'smart' munitions in the war had a 90 per cent success rate against enemy targets.

'As it swooped down to hit the convoy the Iraqis opened up with an anti-aircraft gun'

'An hour or so before last light an F-15E screamed over the target area, pulling high into the grey sky as it passed the convoy. I thought the pilot had taken a flypast as I couldn't see or hear anything – then there was a ball of flame and a thud as the high-explosives detonated. It was strange to see it all unfold, it was just like being at the movies. Everything seemed to happen in slow motion. A second F-15 joined the attack, and as it swooped down to hit the convoy the Iraqis opened up with an anti-aircraft gun, but their efforts were wasted. After a third

feared I might start singing like a canary, and that was one of the main reasons that we were only told what we needed to know.'

As the Scud convoy was making no apparent moves to go anywhere, the SAS team radioed for

strike the whole convoy was decimated, and flames flickered from all the vehicles and smoke billowed into the darkening sky. Their war was over. Nothing moved – we presumed all the Iraqis had been either killed or wounded.'

The other SAS columns were also having good hunting in the desert. On 5 February, for example, A Squadron's Group 2 spotted a Scud convoy of two launchers and four escort vehicles, and immediately called down an air attack. The column later fought a gun battle with a force of Iraqis defending an observation tower, killing 10 of the enemy for no losses. Three days later D Squadron called down an air attack on an Iraqi 'Flat Face' radar installation. On the same day a team from A Squadron destroyed a microwave communications tower, then fought a 40-minute firefight with Iraqi troops before escaping into the wide expanse.

The majority of SAS attacks upon Scud convoys were conducted at long ranges

The worst encounter for the SAS occurred on 9 February, when a small patrol from A Squadron probed an enemy communications centre near Nukhayb. In a heavy firefight the SAS force was beaten off, though not before the patrol leader, a sergeant-major, was badly wounded. He had to be left by the other two and was captured. However, he survived the war and was awarded the Military Cross for his bravery.

The majority of SAS attacks upon Scud convoys were conducted at fairly long ranges – the teams did not want to get too close to an enemy who invariably outnumbered them. The preferred method of destroying the Scud convoys was by calling down an air attack, although if this was not available then the SAS Land Rovers

would attempt it themselves. Typically, the attacks were conducted using vehicle-mounted Milan anti-tank missiles. The following is an account of one such attack:

'When we were within 600m [655 yards] we could identify the target... The next moment several Milan missiles streaked across the desert and slammed into the enemy vehicles. A fireball engulfed the Iraqis as explosives combined with fuel to form a lethal cocktail.'

Such encounters, and the frequent firefights that erupted afterwards with pursuing Iraqis, naturally sapped ammunition and fuel supplies. The Regiment had to find a way to replenish those supplies. To service the vehicle teams, the SAS organised supply columns to drive into Iraq and liaise with its teams in country. These columns consisted of 10 four-ton trucks manned by SAS soldiers and Royal Electrical and Mechanical Engineers (REME) personnel. Six armed Land Rovers from B Squadron made up the escort, and the supply column was named E Squadron. It crossed the border on 12 February and rendezvoused with the Land Rovers from A and D Squadrons 145km (90 miles) inside Iraq. By 17 February it had returned, though not before it had spotted an enemy observation post and had used a laser rangefinder to direct an air attack upon it – this was the first and only time the SAS used a laser designator in the Gulf War.

The teams inserted by helicopter for foot operations inside Iraq were also extracted and supplied by helicopter. The conditions were often far from ideal, though:

'Ammunition, water and radio batteries were quickly divided up and the sandbags tied'

'The weather was getting worse and our big fear was that we were going to tab a fair distance and then discover that the cab [helicopter] couldn't land. As we pulled on our bergens it started to piss down – terrific! There is nothing quite like rain and a strong wind to sap your strength. We had moved off on a bearing and had to use the GPS constantly due to the fact that we could not see a thing. After four hours it had stopped raining, leaving us with damp clothes, which had to dry out while we were wearing them.'

To minimise the risk of compromise, all insertions and extractions were carried out at night where possible: 'We were to be picked up between 0300 and 0400 hours. The pilots would be flying at low level wearing night vision goggles and with all lights off, requiring maximum skill to avoid unmapped obstacles in their way, such as pylons.'

To a team waiting on the ground, cold and wet and with the enemy all around, there is nothing quite like the sound of an in-coming friendly chopper:

'We heard the clap, clap of the Chinook's twin rotors as it came in to land. No one said anything, but I think we all wished we could turn the noise down to avoid alerting anyone in the vicinity of our presence. We had a small strobe which could be held in the hand, and which transmitted a tiny but powerful flashing light. It was ideal in places like South Armagh, where there are plenty of hills, but in the flat Iraqi desert we were worried that the light might be seen. On each side of the strobe, two of us held torches with red filters. As soon as the aircraft came in a crewman flashed a green light from the right-hand door and we put our lights out. We raced to the crewman's door and grabbed the ammunition from him, as well as other stores all packed in sandbags. This is standard SOP, as the sandbags can be useful to a patrol and don't become just rubbish. The crewman wanted to know if we were OK. We gave him the thumbs-up, then we threw in a bag of rubbish from our early morning scoff, as well as the bulging shit bag. We knew someone would have to check the bags before they were thrown away and were they in for a shock! Ammunition, water and radio batteries were quickly divided up and the sandbags tied to the bergens. The most welcome was the fresh rats [rations] – the lads had sent out

Above: One of the most potent ground-attack aircraft used by the Coalition in the Gulf, and used to support SAS missions: the American A-10 Thunderbolt. Its 30mm Gatling gun could rip apart enemy vehicles in seconds.

loads of sandwiches and fresh fruit, which we would trough later.'

Re-supplied, the SAS continued to enjoy success against the enemy. On 18 February, for example, a D Squadron patrol discovered a Scud convoy and called down an air attack to wipe it out. The next day another SAS-directed air attack hit a second convoy. Tragedy struck on 21 February, however, when a running battle developed between a group of Iraqis and one of A Squadron's fighting columns. As the SAS vehicles were pulling back, Lance-Corporal David Denbury was shot and fatally wounded. Nevertheless, the SAS was making a valuable contribution to the battle against the Scuds.

What about the Americans? Delta Force had been concentrating its efforts on several hundred square kilometres of enemy territory around H2 and H3. Typically, the US élite teams would consist of between 20 and 40 commandos, who would mount patrols of between 10 and 15 days in length. Their mission was primarily one of surveillance: watching for any military traffic and calling down air attacks. The results were excellent: by late February US intelligence had con-

cluded that the Scud launchers had been pushed into a small area 16km (10 miles) in diameter around Al Qaim.

Farther east, the Americans had less success in their hunt for Scuds. A number of Green Beret teams were sent into enemy territory to hunt for the missiles. In early February 1991, three were inserted near the town of As Salman. However, two were compromised and extracted almost immediately, while the third spent 30 hours in

SCUD HUNTING

Left: A destroyed Iraqi column. This one was caught near Kuwait City, but it illustrates what air strikes could do, especially when the aircraft were given accurate coordinates by specialist teams, such as the SAS, on the ground nearby.

and medics. In addition, like in the SAS, each man was a crack shot. During their surveillance missions the men lived in the ground in 'hides'. They covered the frames for their holes with hessian, which was then camouflaged. Human waste was bottled and bagged, and like the SAS the men carried bergens filled with loads weighing up to 100kg (220lb).

Although the Green Berets carried out valuable deep reconnaissance behind enemy lines just prior to the Coalition ground offensive, success eluded them in the great Scud hunt. The laurels belonged to the SAS and Delta Force, and Downing telephoned Massey at the end of February and they congratulated themselves for 'establishing Anglo-American dominion over western Mesopotamia.'

It was true that the SAS had not completely stopped the launch of Scud missiles from western Iraq against Israel, but it had made a major contribution in cutting them down severely. From an average of five launches per day during the first week of the war, the figure then fell to less than one launch per day. With the SAS fighting teams on the ground and the US Air Force in the air flying 75-150 anti-Scud sorties per day, the Iraqis found it almost impossible to set up and fire their surface-to-surface missiles. Above all, it had been the British special forces soldiers on the ground who made the biggest contribution to the anti-Scud war. The men who wore the Winged Dagger had once again proved that they were second to none.

hostile terrain but failed to spot any launchers. The Green Beret A Teams were very similar to their SAS counterparts. The A Team itself usually consisted of six to 10 men, and had a skills blend of engineers, communications specialists

CHAPTER 7

Hitting Saddam Where It Hurts

The Allied air campaign effectively destroyed the Iraqi Air Force and Saddam Hussein's air defence network. It also wrecked a large part of his communications network. However, buried landlines containing fibre-optic cables could not be destroyed by air strikes alone, and so Allied special forces units, such as the British SAS, were sent in to locate them and render them useless. It was a dangerous and often frustrating task.

Two aspects of the SAS's war in the Gulf are extremely well known. The first is the campaign in western Iraq against the Scud missiles that were being launched against Israel. The second is the SAS road watch patrols that were mounted in enemy territory. However, the SAS carried out other important missions during the Gulf War, and this chapter examines one of them: the war against the Iraqi communications network.

At the start of the war Iraq possessed considerable air defence and electronic warfare (EW) capabilities, and these had to be immediately reduced if the Coalition was to avoid heavy aircraft losses during the air campaign. In addition, Iraqi air strength had to be reduced. The Iraqi Air Force itself numbered some 750 combat aircraft, ranging from the state-of-the-art Mikoyan-Gurevich MiG-29 'Fulcrum' to the rather aged MiG-21 'Fishbed', both supplied by the USSR. The aircraft in themselves did not pose a major threat: after all, the Coalition had over 2000 combat aircraft to throw at them. If it came to a fight, the Iraqis would be literally shot out of the skies. However, Saddam Hussein's air defence network was another matter. Some 17,000 surface-to-air missiles (SAMs) and 9000–10,000 anti-aircraft artillery pieces defended Iraqi air space. The air defence system's

Opposite: A British Chinook helicopter, similar to the one that was used to insert the SBS team on the mission described in this chapter.

radar networks were fibre-optically connected to integrate the computer data link system, with its command and control links located throughout the country. In addition, for increased survivability, most of the primary command and control nodes were buried and covered in concrete, thus creating hardened shelters. These had to be destroyed quickly to ensure the success of the air campaign.

An essential part in guaranteeing victory in the Gulf was the Coalition's mastery of EW techniques. Broadly speaking, EW involves the use of equipment, techniques and methods intended to ensure the use of the electromagnetic spectrum for communications, surveillance and weapon control, plus the denial of those uses to the enemy. Coalition EW systems were there-

fore vital to the success of the war in the Gulf, and effectively disrupted Iraq's command, control, communications and intelligence system.

The first 14 hours of the air campaign witnessed 1000 sorties flown against Iraq's early warning system, fighter defence direction system, command and control structure and communications network: 80 per cent of these sorties were successful. That is, eight out of 10 aircraft reached their targets, delivered their ordnance and returned home. To destroy Iraqi command, control, communications and intelligence (C³I) facilities, the Coalition employed hard-kill weapons, electronic signal monitoring (the passive interception, identification and analysis of enemy radar and radio signals), and electronic countermeasures (EW techniques and equipment intended to degrade the performance of enemy radars, radio transmitters and weapon-guidance systems). First to be targeted were Iraqi anti-aircraft systems, and during the first 10 days of the air war the US Air Force launched over 1000 sorties against them. The principal weapons used by the Allies were AGM-88 HARM anti-radiation missiles and 'Paveway' laser-guided bombs. The High-speed Anti-Radiation Missile (HARM) is designed to inflict maximum damage on enemy radar antennas and unarmoured missile controls. The 'Paveway' is designed to attack hardened point targets, such as bridges, tunnels and command bunkers.

Under this onslaught the Iraqi defences crumbled, literally. The Iraqi Air Force and air defence network never recovered from the initial air strikes, and the Coalition forces soon had mastery of the skies over Iraq and Kuwait. In addition, the Coalition could listen to any communications sent via transmitters, which rendered Iraqi radios useless. The only way Saddam Hussein could talk to his men in the field was via the buried fibre-optic cables scattered throughout his country. As General John Galvin, Supreme Allied Commander Europe, remarked: 'Schwarzkopf was able to dismantle the electromagnetic spectrum so that he effectively closed Saddam's eyes and ears. He therefore made Saddam less mobile, less able to react, less able to gain intelligence – basically, less able to orchestrate and put the air, land and sea elements together.'

If the landlines could also be cut, the Iraqi dictator would be totally blind and deaf.

But how could they be found? They could not be identified electronically or visually. The only way to disable them was to send in teams to locate and destroy them. The SAS was one of the Coalition special forces units that was earmarked to target the landlines; indeed, the first briefing that SAS soldiers received when they arrived in Saudi Arabia centred on the vital requirement to cut Iraqi communications to starve the enemy of his command and control capabilities (which is a standard priority for special forces in any modern conflict). It was believed that the landlines were the method by which Baghdad communicated with the mobile Scud launchers teams. Therefore, if they could be knocked out it would effectively render the Scud teams without orders and thus disable them (as noted earlier, initiative is not encouraged in a police state). In addition, the Regiment was also tasked by Riyadh with crippling the network of hi-tech microwave dishes which relayed telecommunication messages across Iraq.

The first unit to get a crack at the enemy communications was the SBS

The first unit to get a crack at the enemy communications was not the SAS but its maritime counterpart – the SBS. During the night of 22 January 1991, two Boeing Vertol Chinook helicopters from No.7 Special Forces Squadron flew over the border and headed for a location 70km (43.5 miles) southwest of Baghdad, to a road along the upper shore of Bahr al Milh. Codenamed Operation 'Maud', the mission involved

SAS GULF WARRIORS

Above: Allied communications equipment near the Saudi-Kuwait border. During the early phase of the war, Specialist Coalition communications teams were located close to the border to monitor Iraqi transmissions from a listening station. The SAS was later sent in to deal with it.

36 members of the SBS and took 90 minutes. It ended in total success, when the men brought back parts of the buried Iraqi communications system. The young former Royal Marines officer who commanded the operation was subsequently awarded the Military Cross.

Meanwhile, the SAS teams prepared to launch their own war against Saddam's communications. As ever, the Regiment took the practical approach to its problems. To back up the explosives they carried, the men also packed bolt croppers, small sledge hammers and heavy gauge wire cutters on the grounds that if the communications towers could not be destroyed by explosives they would have to be crippled manually. The method of insertion was Chinook helicopter, which performed sterling work for the SAS during the whole Gulf conflict. One of the first missions launched against the enemy's

communications almost ended in disaster for the Chinook and its crew, as well as the SAS team on board.

Pilot 'M' and his crew had been detailed to insert a 16-man SAS team deep inside Iraq to recover a communications dish from a remote airfield. The mission was launched at night, and so the pilots wore night vision goggles to fly nap-of-the-earth to reach the target. The trip to the airfield was uneventful: no anti-aircraft fire or Roland low-altitude surface-to-air missiles (SAMs) to contend with. In addition, once on the ground the men expected little trouble as low-level photo-reconnaissance had revealed that there appeared to be no enemy units or activity in the area (pre-flight checks concerning possible hazards along the way are always extensive in an effort to anticipate all potential 'show-stoppers' during the journey). The SAS soldiers crowded in the Chinook's hold thought they were dreaming – they were. As the rear wheels of the twin-engined aircraft touched down an explosion ripped through the cabin, tearing away parts of the landing gear as the blast hit the fuselage and punctured all the tyres.

Aboard the Chinook the SAS team prepared to launch themselves off the back ramp and into what they realised was a minefield. At least the helicopter pilot would then have a reduced pay-load, giving him more of a chance to lift off with the power he had left available to him. However, one of the crewmen gestured to the members of the team to remain where they were, and the pilot pulled full power and lifted off the ground

Below: An example of the damage caused by UN aircraft during the air war. During their efforts against Iraqi communications, SAS soldiers were nervous about being strafed by friendly aircraft, especially when operating near the border.

to get out of the area as quickly as possible. Mercifully, the intelligence reports concerning the enemy were correct: they were nowhere to be seen, and the Chinook was free to limp back to Saudi Arabia. Once back at the SAS's forward operating base (FOB), the helicopter was inspected. No less than 77 holes were counted in its fuselage. The crew were congratulated with cold beers, while the senior pilot was later decorated with the Air Force Cross.

Other SAS missions against enemy communications were conducted using Land Rover vehicles. During the first week of the war, specialist Coalition communications teams which were

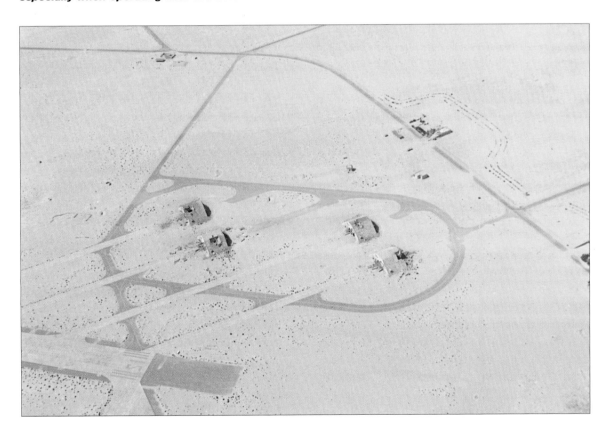

Above: The entrance to an Iraqi underground bunker in Kuwait, like the one destroyed by the SAS team in this chapter. Such positions were often difficult to spot from the air, and so came as a great surprise to SAS teams when they came across them.

working close to the border and constantly monitoring Iraqi transmissions identified what they believed was a permanent listening station that the Iraqis were using to monitor Coalition communications. The site itself could not be identified by aerial photographs. However, it was believed to be very close to the Kuwaiti border, and as such it was decided to send in a mobile SAS unit to deal with it. One of those who took part remembers the feeling of misgivings that the team had about the mission:

'It was like trying to find a needle in a haystack. The intelligence boys had told us that the Iraqi communications unit was less than 60km [37 miles] into Iraq. We managed to pinpoint the area, but we were more than a little concerned that we didn't have any precise information as to its exact whereabouts.'

The Land Rovers were piled high with kit. 'The beauty of a mobile meant that you could take bags of extras, such as sleeping bags. Belt order was always worn, just in case we were bumped and the Rovers were crippled. As a precaution against such a situation, we strapped our bergens on the outside of the vehicles so we could grab them and run in an emergency. Ammunition, food and water was not a problem because we had the vehicles. We had sandbags stocked full of rations, but the most important item was fuel. So we had jerrycans all over the wagons. Everyone wore shemaghs [Arab headdress] and their own personal items of attire. This could be windproof climbing trousers or quilted jackets depending on the weather.

The column consisted of four Land Rover 110 vehicles, all fully armed with Milan anti-tank weapons, 66mm M72 Light Anti-tank Weapons (LAWs), 0.5in Browning heavy machine guns and GPMGs. In addition, Claymore and Elsie anti-personnel mines were also packed. Saudi Arabian special forces were the guides to the border, though it proved to be nothing more than a barren stretch of sand. The SAS soldiers did not have much faith in their Arab counterparts: 'When a Saudi sergeant indicated that we had arrived at the border, we all just looked around in amazement. There was sand, sand and more fucking sand.'

Fortunately the Land Rovers were each equipped with a GPS system, 'which made life much more easier'. However, there was still a danger of being hit by friendly aircraft, so every vehicle carried a Union Jack flag, which was either flown from the radio mast or attached to the bonnet to indicate to Coalition aircraft that these were friendly forces.

By the second day of the mission the SAS still had not located the Iraqi site, although the Regiment's intelligence cell back in Riyadh insisted that the men were in the right area. They were ordered to sit tight and watch. Moving out of the area the team camouflaged their vehicles and established an observation post to survey the terrain, but still nothing happened. On the third day the SAS soldiers spotted two Iraqi trucks arriving from a southerly direction. The trucks stopped and between 10 and 12 enemy soldiers jumped from the vehicles and then seemingly disappeared into the ground:

'After about 10 minutes of deep and serious "where the fuck have they gone" conversation, the boss ordered us to mount up. As usual we were already thinking ahead of him and were packed, ready to leave.'

At this point the SAS soldiers were approximately 3km (1.85 miles) away from the enemy, and the team commander decided to mount a hit-and-run raid. The terrain over which they were operating was appalling, though, which meant they would not be able to monitor the Iraqis while on the move:

'The boss wanted everyone to be ready. We were to go in as fast as possible and hit them hard. His orders had been very clear: "If it looks good we'll go straight in and hope that our sand trail doesn't compromise us."

'Travelling fast and furious in a column of Land Rovers is not SAS standard operating procedure – you give your position away and risk falling into an enemy ambush. Nevertheless, we were confident that the odds were in our favour. Then again, nothing is certain in war.'

'I heard someone utter "good skills" as two more missiles slammed into the trucks'

The SAS team's luck held, though, and the commander's Land Rover came to a halt some 20 minutes later – no one goes anywhere fast over rough terrain. The other vehicles stopped behind it and the men sprang from the 110s. The procedure was second nature:

'I quickly jumped into the back of our Land Rover and unwrapped a makeshift dust cover which we had strapped over the Milan. All four vehicles then manoeuvred into position until they were in a line facing the Iraqi trucks. The gap between each Land Rover was approximately 100m (109 yards).

The team commander flicked the safety catch off the Browning heavy machine gun on his vehicle and let fly with tracer fire at the targets (usually, every fifth round on a belt of ammunition is tracer). Seconds later the Milans screamed towards their targets:

'The power of the missile as it left the weapon pushed a blast of fresh air into our faces and sent stones flying behind us as the backblast. flashed into the desert. I heard someone utter "good skills" as two more missiles slammed into the trucks. Within 45 seconds it was all over. Smoke poured from the remains of the vehicles and the boss opted to carry out a quick inspection of what was left.'

The members of the SAS team felt very pleased with themselves

---

Two vehicles drove down to the site, which was less than 500m (545 yards) down a slope to the front, while the other two remained behind. A short while later small-arms fire was heard coming from the enemy site, though nothing could be seen. This naturally made the men in the two vehicles left behind very anxious. The reconnaissance party then raced back to share some good news with their comrades. It transpired that the Iraqis had constructed their communications bunker underground, hence the inability of the SAS team to spot it, and the trucks had been carrying visiting signallers, who were about to undertake some form of work. The Iraqis were now all dead, but the bunker had been so well constructed that it had proved hard to destroy. Undeterred, the SAS men had manually wrecked everything they could and recovered as much sensitive hardware as possible, before putting in place every piece of explosive they had.

The SAS recovered three Iraqi code books, though it was not known if they were still rele-

vant (it is standard NATO practice to change codes weekly, and during the Gulf war British units changed their codes every 24 hours – it was assumed the Iraqis had a similar procedure). The members of the team naturally felt very pleased with themselves, and also vowed never to criticise Coalition intelligence again – or at least not until the next mission.

Seconds later there was a muffled explosion as the charges went off, sending a cloud of debris and smoke high into the air. A last thud signalled the detonation of the final charge, as a flash of flame darted from the fractured roof of the bunker. The SAS was taking no chances. As there was a chance that something might be left intact, an air attack was ordered on the radio. Around 20 minutes later two American F-15 Eagles swooped down and dropped bombs on the Iraqi bunker. It was time for the SAS team to head home. The journey back was uneventful, the Iraqis having seemed to have gone to ground. The SAS soldiers even had time to stop and have a brew.

The destruction of the entire Iraqi communications network was impossible

---

Elsewhere the SAS hit Iraqi communications facilities wherever they were found. For example, SAS teams blew up seven signal booster stations along the Baghdad-Amman highway. Not all enemy communications were destroyed, however, and the Iraqis still managed to communicate with the mobile Scud teams and with the Republican Guard in Kuwait (mainly by secure landlines). The problem for Allied intelligence units was that landlines themselves cannot be pinpointed and jammed by Electronic Warfare teams because they do not produce an emission when operating. The only way to cripple them was by destroying them. In truth, the destruction of the entire Iraqi communications network by the SAS was impossible, especially as it is a relatively small-sized unit. In addition, the hunt for the Scuds in western Iraq diverted manpower away from the battle against the enemy communications. That said, the SAS did achieve one notable success with regard to hostile communications. SAS teams brought back enemy electronic kit, which was subsequently examined by Coalition specialists. It was found to be first-

class, with frequency hopping capabilities. This caused much concern within the Coalition High Command, which believed it might cause problems during the United Nations ground offensive. Fortunately, the intelligence gleaned from examining captured communications equipment was quickly absorbed and plans amended accordingly. This was a notable victory for the Special Air Service, and will be discussed in more detail in the next chapter.

Below: Iraqi prisoners of war. Where possible, SAS teams operating behind the lines in the Gulf endeavoured to take enemy prisoners. Captured personnel could provide invaluable intelligence.

CHAPTER 8

Intelligence Gatherers

Sitting in camouflaged observation posts deep behind enemy lines and observing enemy troop movements is one of the SAS's wartime tasks. In the Gulf War, however, the Regiment tried its hand at different types of intelligence gathering, such as seizing prisoners and secret Iraqi equipment, and collecting information from a source in occupied Kuwait City itself. As ever, the SAS proved itself to be more than capable of fulfilling these responsibilities.

Intelligence is a vital part of any war. Intelligence concerning production of war material, about the morale of the opposition's servicemen and civilian population, about the disposition of units in the field, about the stocks of ammunition held by enemy frontline units, and so on. Anything that can be used to build the 'big picture' regarding the opposition is extremely valuable and can be potentially war-winning. The gathering of information is a fine art, and those who carry it out, be they spies or soldiers, are usually highly trained. The SAS, as mentioned earlier, is essentially an intelligence-gathering unit. Inserted deep behind enemy lines, small-sized SAS teams are trained to sit for days and weeks in camouflaged hides and gather information about the enemy's movements, dispositions and anything else that is useful to the war effort. This was the task carried out by the Regiment during the 1982 Falklands War, and it would have been its mission during any military confrontation between NATO and the Warsaw Pact on the European mainland.

When Iraq invaded Kuwait in August 1990, the Coalition hoped to gather intelligence from a number of sources regarding the enemy's strengths and weaknesses. As the crisis developed, and it became apparent that the

Opposite: US satellite communications kit in the Gulf. The Americans had the hardware, but the SAS was unimpressed when it came to the accuracy of some US intelligence reports.

Above: A sand table of the Kuwaiti coastline constructed by the Allies. Despite their satellites and photo-reconnaissance, the UN had serious intelligence shortfalls regarding the enemy, which units such as the SAS tried to make up.

Iraqis would have to be forcibly removed from Kuwait, these sources revealed themselves to be disappointing in many respects. For example, it was hoped that satellite imagery would provide reliable information concerning the strengths and dispositions of Iraqi units. It was soon realised that this would not be the case. For example, American analysts were forced to reassess their estimates about the enemy when it was realised that there were six not eight artillery tubes in an Iraqi artillery battery, and that each enemy armoured platoon in fact had four not seven tanks. Satellite imagery also proved inadequate when it came to tracking enemy units as they moved around or mingled with other units. Photographs taken by UN reconnaissance aircraft should have been used to back up satellite imagery, but Washington, reluctant to trigger the outbreak of war prematurely, forbade Coa-

lition aircraft to fly over the Kuwaiti theatre before 17 January 1991. In any case, even when reconnaissance aircraft were finally allowed to fly over Iraq and Kuwait, the Iraqis proved adept at camouflage and concealment, further muddying the waters.

The efforts of the Americans to estimate Iraqi strength on the ground did not impress individual members of the SAS: 'The Americans were piss poor when it came to the enemy's order of battle. In January they thought Saddam had 35 divisions in Kuwait at first, this gradually rose to 40 and then 43. It really didn't reinforce our faith in the intelligence-gathering process.'

It was a fact that the Coalition had large gaps when it came to intelligence. Photographic and signals intelligence could not give an accurate picture of enemy deployments on the ground in Iraq and Kuwait, much less the morale of the Iraqi troops themselves. What was needed was human intelligence (HUMINT), but this was sadly lacking.

Iraq was, and remains, essentially a police state. Rule is enforced through fear, and everyone is encouraged to spy upon his or her neighbour. Thus no one is sure who is watching whom. This makes it very difficult for agents to operate. This being the case, it was almost impossible for the Coalition to get an accurate picture of the mood of Saddam Hussein and his government, the morale of the Iraqi army, or the general mood of the population as a whole. This meant it was almost impossible for Riyadh to determine how the Iraqi troops would react when the ground war began.

The Coalition expected an army of deserters to flood into Saudi Arabia once the air campaign began. This expectation was backed up by a psychological warfare campaign, which included dropping many thousands of bottles off the Kuwaiti coast, each one containing a paper showing US Marines invading the country; 'Voice of the Gulf' radio, which broadcast propaganda; and the thousands of leaflets dropped on enemy troops to encourage them to give themselves up. The results of this exhaustive campaign were minimal: very few deserters came across, and those who did were closely guarded by the Saudi Arabians. The latter allowed questions to be put to the deserters, but no Westerners were allowed to directly question them. From an intelligence point of view this was a complete disaster, as any information obtained was diluted and outdated.

The reasons for the lack of deserters are not hard to find. For one thing, the Iraqi conscripts, for the most part deliberately misinformed, did not know who they were fighting. Iraqi government-controlled propaganda had not exactly painted a rose picture of the Coalition forces. Far more importantly, there were Iraqi execution squads roaming the rear areas of their forces, looking for deserters and tending to shoot first

and ask questions later. Even if a deserter managed to make it to the Coalition lines, he would do so in the certain knowledge that members of his family would be shot in reprisal for his actions. Little wonder that most Iraqi conscripts, tired and hungry, stayed in their foxholes, where many were to die during the war.

'The lifeblood of successful operational deployments is good intelligence'

The British SAS prepared in its own way to fight the intelligence war, as one trooper remembered: 'The lifeblood of successful operational deployments is good intelligence. The sources must be handled by experienced teams who can quickly evaluate the value of available information provided – spoof intelligence can send friendly forces straight into a trap.'

Good, hard intelligence can also be recovered in the form of equipment, which provides an insight for specialists to determine enemy capabilities. In addition, codes and secret battle orders are also vital to the intelligence war. Coalition special forces conducted a masterful side-show during the Gulf War, gathering intelligence and mounting a series of raids that retrieved a valuable haul of enemy equipment.

One human source of intelligence for the Coalition was the conquered Kuwaiti population, though the occupying Iraqi forces were quick to quell any 'subversion'. The Coalition tried to tap into this pool. When the Iraqi Army rolled into Kuwait many policemen went underground and joined resistance units, while some Kuwaiti military personnel tried to hold-up and use satellite telephones to talk direct to the Coalition allies in

Saudi Arabia. However, such high frequencies were quickly detected and located by Iraqi direction-finding teams, who had been trained by Western specialists during the eight-year war with Iran. The 12 satellite communications systems that went underground in August 1990 were quickly seized by Saddam's secret police. Therefore, the Coalition had to put its own units into occupied territory.

'The SAS sought reliable and regular sources of intelligence about Iraqi forces'

US Special Forces had been able to put a forward intelligence team, all of Arab extraction, into Kuwait to join with resistance leaders and prepare for the eventual liberation of the country. At first, though, the Special Operations unit could do little during the early days of the occupation because of the activities of Iraqi troops, who mounted continual house searches in their efforts to find resistance groups. Therefore, the members of the unit kept detailed logs of Iraqi military activity and strengths. Later they managed to locate a team of Kuwaiti resistance fighters who were able to get messages out of Kuwait City via a radio enthusiast, who had already begun working for Coalition intelligence agencies from his cellar.

'The SAS sought reliable and regular sources of intelligence about Iraqi forces inside Iraq. The Regiment had a real find in locating a bloke called Mohammed, a school teacher and computer wizard who had lived in Kuwait all his life and had been a radio ham for more than 10 years. His kit emitted a low pulse and was much more difficult for Iraqi units to target than the

more powerful satellite communications sets, which relied on high-frequency transmission and was easily identified. Mohammed's three computer terminals were linked to a radio transmitter, which he powered by two industrial batteries and a small generator. He sent messages to Europe, to a friendly source in Geneva, and was then passed on to Riyadh.'

Mohammed's information was 'spot on', and after the war he was thanked for his work. At one point he was the only means of 'safe' transmission, and the Iraqis never did locate him. All this work was mostly the preserve of the Americans. For example, two US Special Operations men lived in the attic of a hotel in central Kuwait City throughout the war, from where Kuwaiti resistance fighters would collect messages and take them to Mohammed. This work was, of course, exceptionally high risk but, somewhat ironically, the operation was discovered by journalists when the liberation of the city occurred. The Americans involved duly discounted their role in the war, until the journalists went to visit Mohammed and found that the Americans were sending messages home!

Offshore, US Navy SEALs and Special Boat Service (SBS) personnel landed regularly from small craft and submarines offshore to link up with resistance teams, who were able to feed the Coalition with vital information about where and what the Iraqis were doing inside Kuwait. Both units deployed from submarines, while American units used delivery vehicles to put small teams ashore. The maritime teams were given the task of kidnapping from Kuwait City Iraqi officers who were then ferried back to the fleet offshore and interrogated by experts aboard US aircraft carriers.

Above: An American trainer (right) with Kuwaitis in Saudi Arabia. The Americans put their own men into Kuwait to gather intelligence, though their activities were at first severely curtailed by the Iraqis. All the men were of Arab extraction to blend in as much as possible.

Meanwhile, SEAL teams swam up Kuwaiti beaches to reconnoitre the mine threat, dismantle underwater obstacles and then go ashore to sever fibre-optic communication cables. These teams also recovered detailed information about beach gradients, which provided the vital information for commanders to determine the best amphibious landing sites. In total, more than 8000 US élite troops were on the ground at the height of the war. Of these, at least 20 men died on intelligence-gathering missions, and at the end of the war 11 were listed as missing in action. One Green Beret broke his back when a Chenworth Fast Attack Vehicle turned over after a raid into Iraq to recover Iraqi electronic equipment. The man was evacuated by a Sikorsky UH-60 Black Hawk helicopter of Task Force 160, but the aircraft crashed on the way back, killing all those on board.

In the desert, the SAS carried out missions against Iraqi units that had only one aim: to take prisoners of the highest level. These POWs were driven to a remote rendezvous, from where CH-47 Chinook helicopters airlifted them out and

SAS GULF WARRIORS

transported them back to Saudi Arabia. One of those who took part in these operations records the successes:

'On at least two occasions vital maps and planning papers were recovered. The information was so fresh that the ground commander decided to take advantage of the situation and called in an air strike on the column of Iraqi vehicles marked on the captured map.'

Some of the most spectacular successes in the intelligence war, though, belonged to the SBS. For example, satellite pictures provided perfect details of Kuwait City, allowing Allied intelligence chiefs to map out key reference points for special forces units who would be among the first Coalition troops to enter the liberated city. But while satellite images confirmed that Saddam had dug a trench around Kuwait and filled it with oil ready to create a ring of flame, only special forces could provide the true intelligence picture regarding how deep and how wide the trenches were.

A team of SBS soldier was put ashore and ordered to inspect the trenches. In one of the most heavily populated areas around Kuwait City the SBS buried themselves into the sand and watched the Iraqis by day before moving in close to the trenches at night:

'It was a difficult job. On insertion we were moving less than 100m (109 yards) in front of Iraqi tanks. They were situated on either side of the main highway into Kuwait, just sat there going nowhere – the crews didn't seem to know

what day it was. At first we thought they had put traps in the road, then we realised that the Iraqis had re-routed oil pipes across the desert and across the main road to fill the trenches. Sand bags sat on top of the trenches to allow heavy armour to roll over the pipes, but the whole set-up was very basic. Using night vision goggles to find a route across the sand, we found a good lying-up position and waited for first light. It was obvious almost straight away that although the trenches were 20m (23 yards) wide, the oil had just soaked into the sand. At first we took pictures, measured the trench and waited to bug out that night. The satellite pictures had shown an "oil stain" on the sand, nothing more. It was this

sort of intelligence that allowed Allied commanders to make decisions, knowing full well that Saddam's threats to ignite a ring of fire wasn't going to happen.'

A key source of intelligence was the interception of Iraqi communications at battalion and brigade level, where transmissions were made on mobile sets in a similar style to all military formations. SAS teams, with attached specialists from the Royal Signals, drove into the desert and listened to Iraqi movements (this was impossible with regard to the Republican Guard, which had exercised excellent 'emissions control' as early as 15 September 1990, communicating via secure landlines). For these SAS teams the operations

often ended in frustration, as the signals wizards often found it easier to jam Iraqi transmissions rather than tap into them. These tactics were vitally important, however, for the Coalition had completely underestimated the strength of Iraqi communication regiments. Before the Gulf War, the Iraqis had purchased a series of very advanced radio sets. Fortunately, they had not been able to train their soldiers in their use. As a result, they were not able to use them to their full potential.

The Iraqis also had very strong electronic warfare (EW) capabilities following their procurement just before the war of a major package of advanced electronic kit from a leading European company. This package included frequency

SAS GULF WARRIORS

ections to other support battle groups, and calling in fire support. It could have isolated units from the High Command and possibly cost many more lives. When British Army units took the surrender of thousands of Iraqis during the ground offensive, senior Royal Signals officers were stunned to discover the high standards of EW technology available to Saddam's forces.

An SAS team captured an entire EW squadron during the final days of the war. All the equipment was returned to Saudi Arabia. The entire system was recovered by the British Army and was used to equip a Royal Signals Electronic Warfare unit based in Germany, who since the Gulf War have used it to great effect on exercises. To demonstrate the power of EW, a Royal Signals unit deployed a number of tiny 'one-life' jammers during a battlefield exercise in Germany, in which an artillery unit was playing a key role. Within an hour of the jammers being activated the artillery operation ceased. They had no communications, could not direct their fire, and had in effect been rendered helpless by a team of 16 men with pocket-sized jammers. The demonstration stunned staff officers, who were able to see for themselves the power of EW.

jammers, directional finding equipment and the most advanced listening systems available at that time. The package was delivered to Iraq in two phases, with the equipment delivered first and the training and systems education following. Fortunately for the Allies, the training package was never commissioned, thus the Iraqis had more advanced equipment than the Allies but couldn't use it. Packed in a series of Land Rovers and Land Cruisers, the Iraqis had the capacity not only to listen to Coalition communications, but to also jam all transmissions. The nightmare scenario could have resulted in chaos for the Coalition armoured battle groups in the desert: a successful jam would have prevented units from receiving or transmitting orders, issuing fire dir-

Above: One of the bases from which the SAS conducted its intelligence-gathering missions. Perhaps one of the greatest triumphs for the Regiment during the Gulf War was capturing an entire Iraqi electronic warfare squadron during the final days of the conflict.

Fortunately, during the Gulf War the Iraqis had not been able to utilise their EW capacity to its full extent. In fact, one of the major lessons learned from the experiences of the Gulf War was the importance of EW. For while the computer and the use of electronics may well have increased the efficiency of command communications, the reliance of modern combat units on such methods is now so complete that any disruption, be it through the physical destruction of equipment, or through the more subtle methods of EW jamming, are now quite capable of bringing absolute chaos to an enemy's ranks.

This was just one of the intelligence shortfalls the Coalition experienced in the Gulf. The work of the special forces teams, such as the SAS, aided piecing together the 'big picture', and the Regiment's capture of the Iraqi EW squadron was a major coup. In addition, a joint SAS and American team had confirmed that Saddam had, in the words of one of those who took part, 'a locker full of chemical kit', which resulted in chemical protection for Allied troops being speeded up. For units such as the SAS it proved one thing: nothing beats having men behind enemy lines collecting intelligence.

CHAPTER 9

SAS Gulf War Hardware

Contrary to popular opinion, SAS soldiers are not armed and equipped with space-age gadgetry. The main criteria hardware must meet with regard to SAS use are reliability and robustness. The Regiment prefers to stick to equipment that has been tried and tested in all types of terrain. In the Gulf War, therefore, SAS soldiers were using kit that had been in service for three decades, and in one case a weapon that was in SAS use in North Africa in World War II.

This chapter looks at the weapons and equipment used by the soldiers of the Special Air Service during the Gulf War: why particular weapons and items of equipment were favoured over others, what their strengths and weaknesses were, and how they performed in the conflict.

Before individual items of equipment are studied in detail, it would be worth dispelling a few myths with regard to the hardware used by the Regiment. The first is that SAS men are equipped with 21st-century weapons and kit that is super secret – they are not. For example, the preferred personal weapon in the Regiment is the American M16 assault rifle, a gun that has been 'in the theme park' for over 30 years and is widely available. Nor do SAS soldiers carry James Bond-type wrist watches and microscopic radios on operations. These things work fine in offices and other controlled environments, but they tend to be very delicate and break when subjected to rough handling. The second point is that the Regiment does not have unlimited funds regarding equipment and cannot demand what it wants – the shortage of Claymore mines mentioned in an earlier chapter illustrates the point. It is true that manufacturers seeking SAS endorsement often provide their equipment and clothing to members of the Regiment free of

Opposite: The M16 assault rifle with M203 grenade launcher, the favoured personal weapon combination of SAS soldiers in the Gulf.

SAS GULF WARRIORS

Above: A weapon that has not found favour with the Regiment: the SA-80 assault rifle. The general SAS consensus of opinion regarding this weapon is that it is unreliable – a fatal flaw with regard to special forces equipment needs.

charge, but there are limits to the SAS's annual procurement budget.

Before looking at individual items of kit, we should examine the criteria that hardware has to fulfil in order to be used by the SAS. Essentially, it all boils down to two factors: reliability and robustness. Weapons and other items of kit have to work first time, every time, and in all types of terrain and scenario. It is as simple as that. This is the standard by which everything is judged. The toughest soldiers in the world want equipment that can withstand hard knocks.

So what small arms were used by the SAS in the Gulf, and why? First and foremost was the M16 assault rifle. All modern armies equip their soldiers with assault rifles, and the M16 is one of the most popular models throughout the world, its main rival being the Soviet (now Russian) Kalashnikov family and all its variants. However, in SAS hands the M16 is used very differently compared to its employment in conventional

units. SAS soldiers use their assault rifles for lethal, accurate fire at ranges of generally below 200 metres. Ammunition conservation is uppermost in their minds, especially when operating behind enemy lines. Making every shot count is essential (this is a large part of SAS weapons training), and is one of the reasons why a four-man team can be so devastating in a contact with the enemy. In the M16 the SAS found a weapon that suited its needs.

First used by the SAS in the Borneo conflict (1963-66), the M16 was still in use nearly 30 years later in the Gulf. The reasons for this

Above: The SAS's favourite personal weapon: the M16 assault rifle. Though its 5.56mm round doesn't have the stopping power of the larger 7.62mm bullet, the M16 is light, easy to use and reliable when properly looked after.

longevity are that the weapon is light, is short and fires a 5.56mm round that has a high lethality at short ranges. At longer ranges the weapon's accuracy is suspect, though this does not worry the SAS unduly, as contacts are almost always carried out at short distances.

A more serious drawback with the M16 is its inability to stand up to the sandy conditions

Above: The 5.56mm Minimi light machine gun, as used by the patrol members of 'Bravo Two Zero'. Substantially lighter than the GPMG – 11kg (24lb) compared to 6.8kg (15lb) – it can use either a box magazine or belt feed without alteration.

encountered in the desert. One would assume that this presented problems for SAS soldiers in the Gulf. However, not one of the men the author spoke to referred to difficulties he had with his M16. The reason is obvious: SAS soldiers strip and clean their weapons on a regular basis. In fact, the gun was originally sold as a self-cleaning weapon. However, it was quickly dis-covered that the gas passages had to be cleaned every day to prevent fouling – no weapon is self-cleaning! Nevertheless, the M16 performed well enough in the Gulf and the men themselves had no complaints. One major advantage it has over the earlier 7.62mm Self-Loading Rifle (SLR) in British use is its lighter weight and its lightweight ammunition – important factors for long-range foot patrols.

Why did SAS soldiers in the Gulf not use the shorter 5.56mm SA–80 assault rifle, the standard-issue infantry personal weapon of the British Army, which was used by UK conventional units in Arabia? First of all the M16 is lighter, endearing it more to foot patrol work. Other points in the M16's favour are given by B Squadron's Sergeant Andy McNab:

'The Regiment tried SA-80s in jungle training when they came out, and found it not best suited to its requirements. With the M16 everything's nice and clean, there are no little bits and pieces sticking out. The safety-catch is very simple and can be operated with the thumb – with the SA-80 you have to use your trigger finger, which is madness. If you're in close country with the M16 you can flick the safety-catch off easily with your thumb, and your finger is still on the trigger. What's more, if the safety-catch will go to Automatic on your M16, you know it's made ready: this means it is cocked, with a round in the chamber. You see people patrolling with their thumbs checking the safety-catch every few minutes; the last thing they want is a negligent discharge within earshot of the enemy.'

Like most assault rifles the M16 has single-shot and three-round burst facilities

In addition, like most modern assault rifles the M16 has single-shot and three-round burst facilities (the SA-80 doesn't have the latter), firing modes ideally suited for conserving ammunition.

If the Regiment has stuck to old favourites with regard to assault rifles, there has been a subtle change with regard to patrol machine guns. The General Purpose Machine Gun (GPMG) and heavier Browning 0.5in are still used on SAS vehicles, but the foot teams have opted for lighter models. In the Gulf, for example, 'Bravo Two Zero' carried Belgian 5.56mm Minimis,

not GPMGs because the Minimi weighs only 6.8kg (15lb) compared to nearly 11kg (24lb) of the GPMG, and its smaller-calibre ammunition weighs less, too. The Minimi has a plastic butt, pistol grip and a large plastic handguard, and there is a 'para' version that has a telescopic butt and shorter barrel. One thing that makes the weapon ideal for special forces units is that there is a second feed slot located below the first on the left side of the receiver. Belt-fed ammunition is normally fed into the first slot, but if there is none available, then any M16-type magazine can be fitted into the second feed slot. This interchangeability is a great bonus for elite teams that have to operate behind the lines.

'As you're patrolling the box is across your body, it can bang against you and fall off'

There were other reasons why the SAS used Minimis. As McNab has related: 'The weapon is so light that it can be used in the attack like a rifle, as well as giving support fire, and it has a fearsome rate of fire. It has a bipod to guarantee good, accurate automatic fire if needed.'

However, the Minimi did have disadvantages: 'The plastic prepacked boxes of ammo for the weapon are not its best design feature. As you're patrolling the box is across your body; it can bang against you and fall off, but you just have to guard against it. Another problem can be that the rounds are not completely packed in the boxes and you get a rhythmic, banging noise, which is bad news at night as noise travels more easily.'

Despite these shortcomings, 'Bravo Two Zero' got good service out of its Minimis, and they were one of the reasons why the patrol managed

Left: In service since the late 1950s, the GPMG is a popular weapon with SAS soldiers. Though it is somewhat heavier than the current crop of 5.56mm machine guns, its accuracy, range, robustness and reliability make it hard to beat.

to kill 250 of the enemy during their escape attempt. However, the patrol suffered one of the perennial problems associated with machine guns carried by foot-mounted patrols: they ran out of ammunition. It is not unknown for a four-man patrol to carry over 1000 rounds of machine-gun ammunition between them, plus more ammunition for each man's personal weapon. This is a back-breaking load, but one that can be easily expended, even using short, controlled bursts, as machine guns have a cyclical rate of fire of anything up to 1000 rounds per minute. This is what happened to 'Bravo Two Zero' and it is a problem that has yet to be solved.

SAS vehicles in the Gulf bristled with weapons, and chief among them was the GPMG

With the foot patrols carrying Minimis, the venerable GPMG was regulated to vehicle duty. Like in the North African desert 50 years earlier, SAS vehicles in the Gulf War bristled with weapons, and chief among them was the GPMG. This 7.62mm machine gun first entered service in the late 1950s, and is still in SAS employment. Though it is larger and heavier, it has one main advantage over its smaller-calibre counterparts: its range and heavier round means greater lethality at long ranges. In addition, the GPMG is very reliable: it works in all terrain types and can take a lot of punishment. When SAS soldiers armed with GPMGs have a clear field of fire, the effects

can be devastating. The following account is from one of the Regiment's soldiers who took part in the Loughall ambush in 1987, when the SAS shot and killed eight members of the Irish Republican Army in an ambush, but is just as relevant to the Gulf as Northern Ireland: 'Bullets were spraying everywhere. By this time everyone was directing their fire at the van [in which the terrorists arrived], and it was taking so many hits that I thought it would disintegrate... Empty cartridge cases were flying all over the place, and in the background I could hear the rippling firing pattern of the GPMGs. I knew whoever was in the van would be dead for certain.'

The GPMGs proved once again that they were robust, reliable and accurate

Mounted on SAS Land Rovers, the GPMGs proved once again that they were among the most robust, reliable and accurate machine guns in the world. The vehicle-mounted teams that operated in Iraq during the war were always careful not to get drawn into close-quarter firefights with the Iraqis. Fortunately, the range of the GPMGs (up to 1800m [1975 yards] in the sustained-fire role) meant that firefights could be conducted at a safe distance (the new generation of light squad machine guns tend to have somewhat shorter ranges: up to 1000m [1095 yards]).

Another machine gun that was used by SAS Land Rover patrols was the American Browning

0.5in model, a weapon that has been used by the Regiment since World War II. The reason why this weapon has not been phased out of service is simple: it is a fearsome machine gun that is easy to operate and is also accurate. In addition, its 0.5in round can penetrate over 40mm (1.6in) of armour at ranges of over 800m (875 yards), and the gun itself has an effective range of 1800m

(1975 yards). With its steady rate of fire of 450–575 rounds per minute, the weapon delighted SAS teams in the Gulf with its ability to disable almost anything moving that it came across.

The following is an account from an SAS soldier of an attack mounted against an Iraqi column that took place in January 1991: 'A steady and well-aimed stream of SAS GPMG and

Left: Mounted on SAS Land Rovers in the Gulf War, the Milan anti-tank weapon was also very effective against Iraqi bunkers. As well as being accurate and having good armour penetration, Milan also has an excellent night sight.

mount. One disadvantage with earlier Brownings was that when the barrel was changed the headspace (the tiny gap between the bolt face and the rear of the barrel when the bolt is closed) had to be reset for the new barrel, which was a time-consuming and very awkward operation on missions. However, SAS Brownings have quick-change facilities, doing away with the need to alter the headspace. With its ability to tackle aircraft and light armoured vehicles, the Browning is so suited to SAS vehicle operations that it will be used well into the next century. There is nothing on the horizon that remotely comes close to bettering it – a remarkable testament to a weapon that was a World War I concept.

Generally speaking, SAS foot patrols cannot carry the heavier infantry weapons

These, then, were the small arms used by the regiment in the Gulf, a blend of the old and the new, but all tried and tested in many different theatres and in different conflicts.

Conspicuous by its absence is the handgun currently used by the Regiment: the Browning High Power. There is a very good reason for this: it fires 9mm rounds, which would have meant SAS soldiers and teams carrying ammunition of another calibre, which translates into additional weight. SAS foot patrols in the Gulf were already over-burdened with weight; the last thing they needed was additional bulk.

Browning 0.5in rounds poured into the Iraqi position as the camp began to catch fire. I didn't know what was burning, but it made an excellent point of reference for the gunners.'

Photographs of SAS Land Rovers in the Gulf reveal that the Brownings were mounted in conventional fashion: ammunition held in a steel box which was clipped to the side of the gun

SAS GULF WARRIORS

What of support weapons? Generally speaking, SAS foot patrols cannot carry the heavier infantry weapons, such as mortars and field pieces. Despite the fact that such weapons can substantially increase the firepower of a team, and are often invaluable in the defensive role, weight considerations rule them out. For vehicle-mounted teams, however, it is different, and during the Gulf War, Land Rover patrols employed a variety of support weapons, chief among them being the Milan anti-tank weapon.

Milan is designed to be used by infantry from a defensive position. It fires a semi-automatic command to line-of-sight (SACLOS) wire-guided missile, which means the operator has to keep

Above: Another weapon that was mounted on SAS vehicles in the Gulf was the American M19 40mm grenade launcher, an air-cooled, machine-gun type weapon that can fire a variety of grenades up to a range of 1600m (1750 yards).

the cross-hairs of the weapon's sights on the target throughout its flight. The missile system itself weighs over 16kg (35lb) including the 6.65kg (14.7lb) missile, making it totally impractical to be carried by a foot patrol. Mounted on Land Rovers, though, the system was extremely potent. Having a range of 2000m (2185 yards) and able to penetrate up to 1060mm (41.75in) of armour, Milans wrought havoc upon Iraqi vehicle convoys.

SAS soldiers themselves are fond of Milan, which is 'a fucking good piece of kit' in general parlance. One of those who took part in the mobile fighting columns in January and February describes a typical Milan engagement: 'The next moment several Milan missiles streaked across the desert and slammed into the enemy vehicles. A fireball engulfed the Iraqis as explosives combined with fuel to form a lethal cocktail.'

Grenade launchers are now highly favoured by special forces units

The Milans were particularly useful during the 'great Scud hunt' in western Iraq (see relevant chapter). The procedure was for an SAS patrol to request an air attack when a team had spotted a Scud convoy. However, the process could be tortuous, for the team reported the Scud to Riyadh, where the US Tactical Aircraft Control Center then passed on the details to an AWACS aircraft, which then vectored a Fairchild Republic A-10A Thunderbolt II or McDonnell Douglas F-15E Eagle onto the target: this could take nearly an hour in total. Thus the fighting columns often used their own Milans instead of calling in an air attack. The Milans also had two additional advantages for the SAS: they are difficult to detect in battle as a result of their reduced noise and flash compared to similar systems, and being wire-guided they are not vulnerable to electronic countermeasures.

A further support weapon that was mounted on SAS Land Rovers during the Gulf War was the American M19 grenade launcher. Grenade launchers are now highly favoured by special forces units, and the reasons are obvious. A grenade launcher can throw a projectile over a distance of up to 1600m (1750 yards). In addition, because they fire fragmentation projectiles, as opposed to point weapons such as bullets, they are regarded as being useful if a unit is ambushed because it can lay down a large amount of firepower at a moment's notice. Despite the advantages, grenade launchers do have a number of drawbacks. First, the grenade travels in a straight line, unlike a hand grenade which can be thrown over cover: this makes it rather inflexible. Second, because the fired grenade is two-thirds fuse, the punch when it hits is not as great as expected. Third, the grenades lack punch against bunkers and other strongpoints.

The SAS vehicles were thought to be very vulnerable to enemy aircraft

Despite these negative factors, grenade launchers are 'flavour of the month' within the Regiment, especially in its M203 version that can be fitted beneath the barrel of an M16 rifle. The US M19 grenade launcher is essentially an air-cooled, blowback-type machine gun that can fire a variety of grenades, including high-explosive, anti-personnel and armour-piercing. Usually fed from 20- or 50-round magazine containers, they can throw their rounds out to a range of up to 1600m (1750 yards) travelling at a speed of 240m (262 yards) per second.

With a weight of 1.63kg (3.6lb), the M203 grenade launcher is considerably lighter than the 34kg (75lb) M19, and was first used nearly 10 years before in the Falklands. Everyone who served with the Regiment in the Gulf wanted an M203. It was originally developed to overcome the problem encountered with the earlier M79 grenade launcher, which was a dedicated weapon. The requirement for a rifle/grenade launcher package resulted in the M203. It is not hard to appreciate the reasons why the M203 is popular in the Regiment: at a stroke it increases the firepower of a team, and it also gives a patrol behind enemy lines an anti-armour capability. SAS soldiers see little wrong with it, as Andy McNab relates: 'In my opinion the one and only drawback with a 203 is that you can't put a bayonet on because of the grenade launcher underneath.'

Another support weapon that was used by both the Regiment's foot patrols and its Land Rover teams was the American 66mm M72 Light Anti-tank Weapon (LAW). Because it is a throwaway launcher that weighs only 2.36kg (5.2lb), foot patrols can take them along on missions. In battle it is a potent weapon: it can defeat enemy armour up to 335mm (13.2in) thick, is accurate, has a range of up to 300m (330 yards) against stationary targets, and is reliable. With its ability to knock out strongpoints, the M72 was carried

Below: One of the most effective hand-held anti-aircraft surface-to-air missile systems in the world: Stinger. This US weapon was issued to SAS groups in the Gulf War. Its advantage over its rivals is that it is a fire-and-forget missile.

Above: The British equivalent to Stinger: Javelin. The disadvantage of Javelin as far as units such as the SAS are concerned is that the firer has to guide the missile to its target, making him vulnerable to enemy detection.

during the Gulf War and its only disadvantage is its prominent firing signature, though in general the advantages of the weapon definitely outweigh the disadvantages.

For the air-defence role, SAS Land Rover teams carried the American FIM-92 Stinger surface-to-air missile. Because of the nature of the terrain in western Iraq in which they were operating – flat and with very little cover – SAS vehicles were thought to be very vulnerable to being spotted and attacked by enemy aircraft (the Coalition quickly established air supremacy over Kuwait and Iraq, but enemy aircraft, especially armed helicopters, continued to fly throughout the war, especially in Iraq itself). With no cover available, vehicles caught out in the open are sitting ducks. Stinger was the answer. Weighing only 15.8kg (35lb), the Stinger has an advanced passive infra-red guidance system, which means the firer does not have to guide the missile: once he has fired the Stinger he can forget it. Having an onboard identification friend or foe system, the missile will not accidentally shoot down a friendly aircraft, or so the theory goes. In addition, the system itself does not require its opera-

tor to possess a post-graduate degree in physics, thus allowing its widespread distribution among the SAS squadrons. The latest version of Stinger is the Passive Optical Seeker Technology (PO-ST) version, which is designed to be more effec-

tive at low altitudes and is more resistant to infra-red countermeasures. Interestingly, the SAS favours Stinger to the British equivalent, the Javelin. The latter is a lighter (11.1kg [24.5lb]) weapon, which seems to make the choice of the

Methods of insertion are always a problem for special forces teams, and in this the SAS is no different. David Stirling, the founder of the Regiment, insisted that his unit should be able to arrive at its target by sea, air or land, and this has been the guiding principle of the SAS's training ever since. One of the ways to arrive at the target is by vehicle, and by the time of the Gulf War the SAS had 50 years of experience with specially adapted vehicles. The trucks and Jeeps of World War II had given way to Land Rovers in the 1950s, and ever since the SAS has stuck to these tried and tested vehicles.

Land Rovers are probably the most reliable light vehicles in the world

Why are Land Rovers so good? First, they are powerful and agile at low speed in mud and sand, while their road speed is quite good for what is essentially an off-road vehicle. Second, all variants have good power/weight ratios, together with good underbelly clearance. They also have an even weight distribution, which means they retain good control over soft surfaces. Finally, and perhaps most importantly, they can be serviced in the field, and they can take a lot of punishment. They are not perfect by any means, and in many ways SAS Land Rovers are a compromise between payload and speed. Nevertheless, they are probably the most reliable light vehicles

Stinger surprising. However, the Javelin has a SACLOS guidance system (see above description of Milan aiming system for an explanation of SACLOS). SAS troopers do not stand around and present themselves as a target to the enemy!

in the world, and for that reason alone they are worth their weight in gold on operations.

The majority of SAS vehicles of this marque in the Gulf were Land Rover 110s. These vehicles have a 110in (2.79m) chassis with a coil-spring suspension to give a degree of comfort for the passengers. The vehicles themselves were liberally festooned with Jerrycans of fuel, M19 grenade launchers, Browning heavy machine guns, Milan anti-tank weapons (usually secured in place with

Left: A Land Rover 110, similar to the ones used by the SAS in the Gulf. Having a good power-to-weight ratio and even weight distribution, Land Rovers are ideally suited to missions in rough terrain. As such, they meet SAS vehicle needs.

Mention here should also be made of an SAS experiment that failed in the Gulf with regard to light vehicles. The Regiment used, and continues to use, Land Rovers to excellent effect. A rather less successful venture concerned the experimentation with dune-buggies in the Gulf, which really came to nothing and put an end to the SAS use of such vehicles. A trend led by the Americans, such vehicles at first glance seem ideal for special forces missions. For example, they are light enough to be carried slung beneath the fuselage of a helicopter, they are quick once deployed, and because of their size are difficult to spot. In addition, because they are open-framed, they have a reduced thermal and radar signature. On paper these attributes seemed to recommend their immediate use by élite teams. They have several serious drawbacks, however, most notably because their size makes its impossible for them to carry large quantities of food, ammunition, fuel or water – the very things upon which a successful long-range vehicle mission depends. Such vehicles are thus dependent upon continual re-supply, either by aircraft or some other form of supply vehicle. At the end of the day the bad outweighed the good as far as the special Air Service was concerned.

The dune buggy vehicles that were produced for the Regiment, called Light Strike Vehicles (LSVs), were not in themselves poor but merely unsuited to the SAS's operational needs. They had four-wheel drive, an excellent steel chassis, plus facilities to mount a variety of weapons, but

improvised wooden brackets and cord), Stingers and GPMGs, plus all the passengers' personal kit, ammunition, water and food. They were head and shoulders above anything similar deployed by other members of the Coalition.

their range of 400km (250 miles) and payload of 500kg (1100lb) were both found to be wanting. Nevertheless, LSVs were deployed to Arabia and did perform reconnaissance duties along the border. They were, however, never deployed by the Regiment inside Iraq.

The aircraft used to get the men behind the lines was the CH-47 Chinook

---

The Americans, not having a long association with vehicles specifically adapted for special forces needs, did employ dune buggies operationally. The Chenworth Fast Attack Vehicle (FAV) as used by Delta Force in the Gulf has a greater range and payload capacity than the LSV, though neither approaches those of the Land Rover. Delta Force used the FAVs in much the same way that the SAS used its Land Rovers, with one slight difference: because of the range deficiencies of the FAVs, the Americans were restricted to making short-range penetration raids with their vehicles. This suited the Delta Force men on the ground in any case, as US vehicle groups do not like to operate for long distances without air cover. Though Delta Force was successful in the Gulf, an FAV column would still find it impossible to operate for long periods without continual re-supply by helicopter.

Vehicles are one way of getting to the target. Another and considerably quicker way is by aircraft, and ever since its creation the SAS has been closely associated with airborne insertion, first by aircraft and then by helicopter. Despite its training in parachute insertion techniques, they are now rarely used on operations, and there was not one SAS parachute drop in the whole of the Gulf

War. The reason for this was simple: parachute drops are high-risk, and nine times out of 10 teams can be inserted just as effectively by helicopter. The only parachute mission earmarked for the Regiment during the war was the rescue of Western hostages, and there was a huge sigh of relief among the Regiment's soldiers when it was called off: they knew that it would have been a complete fiasco.

Similarly, note the reaction of an SAS soldier from G Squadron during the Falklands War when his unit found out they were going to be dropped by parachute onto West Falkland from a Hercules: 'Stunned silence – we couldn't fucking believe it. OK we had sterile 'chutes, but in the South Atlantic wind there is no way you can make an accurate drop onto a relatively small bit of land after leaving an aircraft at an altitude of 10,000m. Anyway, common sense prevailed and this idea was shelved.'

The aircraft used to get the men behind enemy lines was the CH-47 Chinook, designated Chinook HC.Mk 1 in British Royal Air Force service. These workhorses served the SAS superbly during the Gulf War, and an excellent relationship grew up between the helicopter crews and their SAS passengers. The Chinook has a tandem twin-rotor configuration, and has a ramp at the rear to facilitate loading and unloading. Perhaps the Chinook's greatest asset with regard to SAS missions is its ability to withstand punishment; indeed, its rotor blades are constructed from Nomex and glassfibre and are able to take direct hits from a 23mm cannon round and remain intact. The fuselage can also take a lot of punishment, as one Chinook found when it landed in the middle of an Iraqi minefield, but managed to limp back to base intact. In the Gulf War

Above: The GPS system (held by the pilot left) was a great help to SAS soldiers in the often poorly mapped, featureless landscape of western Iraq. Hand-held GPS receivers gave accurate read-outs of patrols' exact locations.

some Chinooks were equipped with additional fuel tanks to extend their range, and were painted in a special night camouflage pattern to aid their clandestine work.

For most SAS soldiers, transport to the Gulf region itself was by Lockheed C-130 Hercules transport. Once in the theatre, the Hercules provided tactical transport, which included transporting fuel for covert helicopter missions. The C-130s in British service are designated Hercules C.Mk 1 and, with a lengthened fuselage, Hercules C.Mk 3. Their refuelling probes, radar and full wingspan thermal de-icing facilities give them extended range and all-weather capabilities, and means the Regiment's men can be

Above: The GPS system (held by the pilot left) was a great help to SAS soldiers in the often poorly mapped, featureless landscape of western Iraq. Hand-held GPS receivers gave accurate read-outs of patrols' exact locations.

transported to anywhere in the world. In addition, its strengthened fuselage, paddle-blade propellers and multi-wheel tricycle landing gear with large tyres means the aircraft can land and take-off from rough airstrips with heavy loads. Without the use of Hercules aircraft, re-supply of the SAS's forward operating base would have been extremely difficult.

One of the most valued items of equipment used by the SAS in the Gulf War was not a

Left: The PRC319 radio, as currently used by the SAS, is a microprocessor-based tactical radio. It can transmit messages in burst mode, thus making it extremely difficult for enemy direction-finding teams to get a fix on the source.

weapon, vehicle or aircraft. Yet almost every SAS soldier who fought in the war has testified that it was extremely effective, and that without it many missions would have failed. This piece of American kit was the Global Positioning System (GPS). Essentially, GPS consists of a number of satellites in orbit above the Earth. Each satellite orbits the earth twice a day, and all of them transmit precise position and time information on a 24-hour basis. If one has a GPS receiver one can work out one's precise location anywhere on the planet. The receiver determines its position by picking up information from three or more satellites at once (there are 21 and three spares orbiting the Earth at all times) and then calculating the distance between the user and each satellite. It then uses a computation to determine the position of the user, which is then displayed on the receiver.

In the Gulf SAS teams carried Magellan GPS NAV 1000M receivers. They weighed 0.85kg (1.9lb) and measured 210mm x 90mm x 50mm (8.25in x 3.5in x 2in), and were made of high-impact, thermal-formed plastic rubber. To SAS teams on the ground in the poorly mapped area of western Iraq, and with sandstorms, driving sleet and snow and featureless terrain the norm, GPS was a godsend. They were also useful for identifying the precise location of Scud convoys, allowing accurate co-ordinates to be relayed to Riyadh. How accurate? Research has shown that the receivers used by the Regiment in the Gulf were accurate to within 25m (27.5 yards).

The one thing special forces teams deep inside enemy territory need is reliable communications. This is especially true of the SAS, which is tasked with acquiring intelligence and relaying it back to headquarters for immediate dissemination. Without reliable and secure communications, an SAS team in enemy territory is useless. The Regiment has therefore spent a lot of time ensuring its men have reliable and secure communications equipment. The set used by patrols in the Gulf War was the PRC319, a microprocessor-based tactical radio which has burst mode and encryption facilities. The former consists of the radio operator feeding the data to be transmitted into a data entry device. The message is then sent in burst form, which is much faster than voice and is virtually undetectable by enemy electronic signal monitoring (ESM) systems. Encryption devices make it very difficult for the enemy to decipher what is being said.

The wind can freeze flesh in minutes, resulting in frostbite or even death

Several other features of the PRC319 make it ideal for SAS missions, not least that it can withstand salt contamination, rain, dust, immersion in water, and being dropped by parachute. In addition, the battery has a life of 500 hours, thus ensuring that it can last throughout a mission. The PRC319 has been well designed and manufactured, a credit to Thorn EMI. It will remain in SAS use well into the next century.

We have discussed weapons, transportation methods, and radios. That leaves clothing. With the limited space available it would be impossible to list and discuss every item of clothing

SAS GULF WARRIORS

Above: The Claymore anti-personnel mine, favoured by the SAS for missions behind enemy lines. The Claymore fires 350 metal balls over a fan-shaped area up to a range of 100m (109 yards). It can be fired manually or electrically activated by command or trip-wires.

meant cold weather gear, chief among them being Gore-tex smocks. Gore-tex is a 'breathable' material that lets sweat vapour pass through but prevents water from coming in. Protecting the head is all-important on missions, and so in the Gulf many SAS soldiers donned native Arab shemaghs. At the other end of the body, SAS soldiers pay particular attention to the feet, as they have to transport the men on their operations. The high-neck desert boot was favoured in the Gulf, together with jungle boots, depending on individual choice.

The final items of equipment that played a major part in SAS missions were belts and bergens. The belts worn by the men themselves were unremarkable. Of more importance was the things attached to them. Belt kits are an essential part of any SAS man's hardware, and contain all the things he needs to survive when he is on his own. For example, he will carry spare magazines for his personal weapon, a compass, a survival kit, water bottles and a knife. With these pieces of kit he has a chance of living and staying out of the clutches of the enemy. Bergens, of which the SAS favours the 60-litre Cyclops type and 80-litre Crusader varieties, are usually filled with ammunition, food, water and clothing. Other items carried can include spare batteries for the patrol radio, medical kit and explosives. Such loads can often weigh in excess of 100kg (220lb).

worn by SAS soldiers in the Gulf. However, there are some aspects with regard to clothing that should be mentioned. Chief among them is that clothing is vital to the success or failure of a mission. 'Thermal threats' are not underestimated by the Regiment. For example, inadequate clothing in arctic regions can result in flesh being exposed. If this happens the wind can freeze flesh in minutes, resulting in frostbite or even death (two of the members of 'Bravo Two Zero' died of hypothermia in Iraq). Thus the right clothing is essential.

In the Gulf SAS soldiers were faced with a dilemma when it came to clothing. The region was subjected to unusually cold weather conditions, and they had to dress accordingly. This

In the final analysis, it is the man wearing the equipment, firing the weapon or driving the vehicle that is often the difference when it comes to contacts with the enemy. It has always been the calibre of SAS soldiers that has made the difference on operations. This was true in the Gulf, and it remains the case.

The Gulf Region

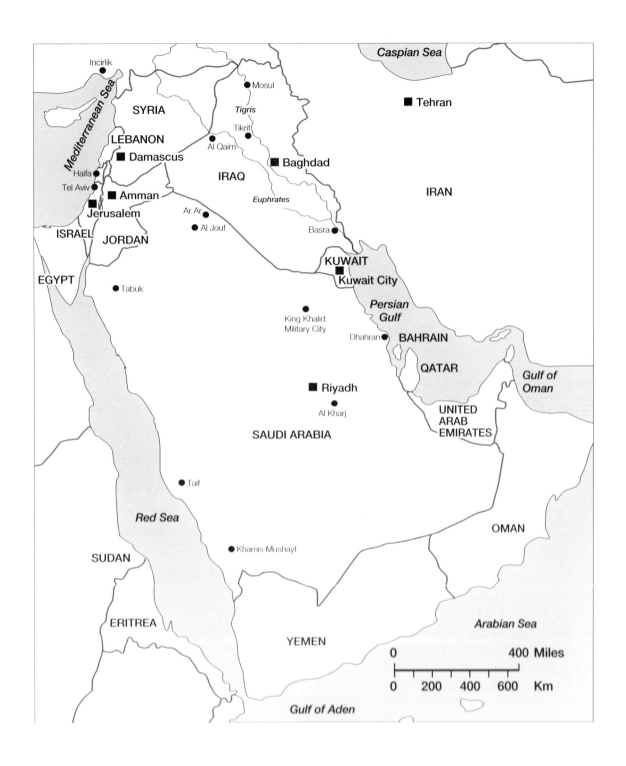

Incirlik

Caspian Sea

Mosul

■ Tehran

SYRIA

Tigris

Tikrit

LEBANON

Al Qaim

■ Damascus

■ Baghdad

IRAQ

IRAN

Haifa
Tel Aviv

Euphrates

■ Amman

Ar Ar

Jerusalem

● Al Jouf

Basra

ISRAEL   JORDAN

KUWAIT

EGYPT

Kuwait City

● Tabuk

Persian Gulf

●
King Khalid
Military City

Dhahran ●   BAHRAIN

QATAR

■ Riyadh

Gulf of Oman

● Al Kharj

UNITED
ARAB
EMIRATES

SAUDI ARABIA

● Taif

OMAN

Red Sea

● Khamis Mushayt

SUDAN

ERITREA

Arabian Sea

YEMEN

| 0 | | | | 400 Miles |

| 0 | 200 | 400 | 600 | Km |

Gulf of Aden

SAS Operations in Western Iraq

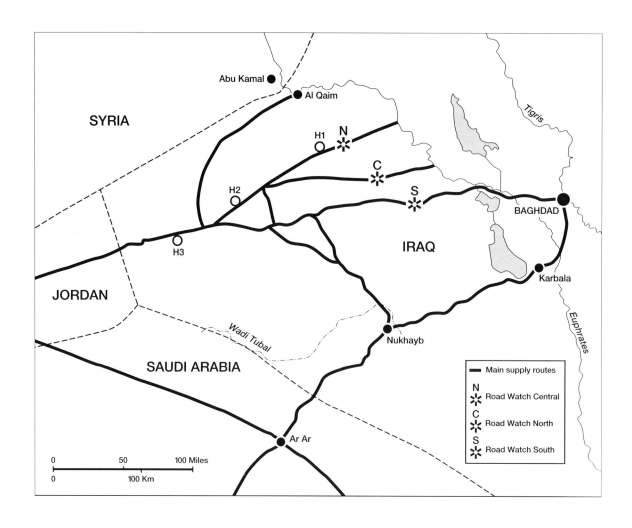

INDEX

INDEX